WHEN A WOMAN MEANS BUSINESS

Debbie Moore was born and raised in the sub-
urbs of Manchester, and left school at fifteen to
become a top international model within a year.

In 1979 she opened the one and only popular
dance centre in London's Covent Garden, developing it into the internationally famous Pineapple, to be quickly followed by other centres and
retail outlets.

Success was such that in 1982 Pineapple
became a public company and Debbie became
the first woman Chairman to walk on the floor
of the Stock Exchange. Four years later she re-
privatized the still-thriving Pineapple business,
making one of the now fashionable management buy-outs.

Debbie Moore lives in London and has one
daughter, Lara.

Acclaim for *When A Woman Means Business*

'Debbie Moore's chatty book tells how she has run Pineapple since she founded it 10 years ago without any business experience at all. It is packed with advice and hints for other women thinking of launching a business of their own.

'Debbie is amazingly resilient and fizzes with energy and optimism. Certainly she has proved that you don't need to be conventional, and knows much better than you or I how many noughts there are in a million!'
GRAHAM LORD, Literary Editor, *Sunday Express*

'The Pineapple boss's new book tells of the rise and rise of her fitness empire, and gives advice and tips to would-be female executives on how to climb the corporate ladder – and reach the top!' ROSS BENSON, *Daily Express*

'*When A Woman Means Business* kept me rivetted from cover to cover! Having studied fashion marketing for 3 years, I thought Debbie said it all in 150 pages. I couldn't put it down.'
SHEENA ROBERTSON, *Sky magazine*

'*When A Woman Means Business* is choc-a-bloc with unpretentiously phrased advice, based on Debbie's experiences and sometimes unconventional view of life.

'The book is an absolute must for everybody – male or female – who plans to found a company!'
DONU KOGBARA, *Girl About Town*

'If you dream of running your own business, don't start planning your empire until you've read Debbie Moore's new book. *When A Woman Means Business* is easy to read, knowledgeable, inspiring and informative.' JACQUI RIPLEY, *19*

'Debbie Moore has learned a trick or two since launching her company Pineapple 10 years ago. Now she has decided the time is ripe to share her wealth of business experience. *When A Woman Means Business* is her story of how to go it alone and win!' *Today*

'Up-tempo, never-say-die stuff! Loads of tips for the aspiring Moore clone. If Moore has a mantra then surely it's "Go For It"!'
JONATHON GREEN, *Books magazine*

WHEN A WOMAN MEANS BUSINE$$

Debbie Moore

FONTANA/Collins

The majority of the photographs which appear in this
book are from the author's private collection, but the
first photograph is reproduced by kind
permission of John Swannell and the last by
Terry O'Neill for *Tatler*.

First published by Pavilion Books Limited
in association with Michael Joseph Limited in 1989

First published in 1990 by Fontana Paperbacks
8 Grafton Street, London W1X 3LA

Printed and bound in Great Britain by
William Collins Sons & Co. Ltd., Glasgow

To my parents – Ron and Hazel Moore

Contents

Introduction

I have lost count of the number of times I've been asked how someone like me who left school at fifteen without an 'O' level to my name, and no business background, could start up and develop a successful business. As we celebrated our 10th anniversary in June 1989, I decided to write *When a Woman Means Business* telling the story of the rise and fall – and rise – of Pineapple, from its modest beginnings as a dance centre, in what had been a disused pineapple warehouse in Covent Garden, to the development of other Pineapples both here and in New York; going public amid lots of razzamatazz in 1982, hitting problems, turning the business around by making acquisitions, to privatizing the business in 1988.

When a Woman Means Business is based not only on my own experiences and the conclusions I've drawn from them, but on those of friends and fellow business-women like Anita Roddick of the Body Shop, Sophie Mirman of the Sock Shop and Christina Smith who has built a business empire in London's Covent Garden.

There's no doubt that women in business have made great strides in the last ten years. It's partly due to a wider acceptance of women in many spheres of activity, while events like the Veuve Clicquot Business Woman of the Year Award (which Anita, Sophie and I have all won) have done a great deal to raise our profile.

We still have a long way to go, but I have no doubt that we will get there in the end. Many of the young women I meet are so full of confidence and energy, not even recognizing the existence of the obstacles that we have had to overcome.

I hope this book will give any woman who means business not only practical advice, but the encouragement and inspiration to achieve success.

I honestly believe that anyone who has a depth of common-sense, a lot of courage and the capacity for very hard work can be successful in business.

I am constantly being told how lucky I am, and as Prime Minister Margaret Thatcher is fond of quoting 'luck is only opportunity meeting readiness', and I must admit the harder I work the luckier I become!

People get fed up of hearing me say that nothing good comes easy, but if you really want the constant challenge and fulfilment of an interesting career, I hope this book will help you to have the courage to have a go.

The confidence you need will come with experience and I hope that reading about mine will get you off to a good start.

Getting Started

Once you've decided that you would like to start a business of your own, ask yourself 'Why?' Is it simply because you're sick of working for someone else? Or because you want to make a million? In both these cases, you should think again. Working for yourself presents just as many problems (if not more) as working for someone else, and at the end of the day, the buck stops firmly with you.

If money is your primary motivation, I think you are finished before you start. Like most of the successful businesswomen I know, I didn't go into business to make a fortune. I was interested in finding something I enjoyed doing, which would also give me a good living. Being in business is tough, and it's much easier to be tough if you enjoy what you do and care about it. The status and money may well come along, but they are only a by-product.

Sophie Mirman, who founded the highly successful Sock Shop chain with her husband Richard Ross, agrees:

'I could never have gone into business saying I want to make a million. That's just not the way I think at all.

When we started, our great ambition was to have four shops in London, and if we were a howling success, maybe six! But you do see new companies now opening their first shop and saying, "We want to open fifty shops and then go public . . .". I think that's a terrible shame. You can't enjoy building up your business if your only interest is the bottom line – the profit. Both Richard and I feel exactly the same. We love the product and if we get that right and develop the business properly, the bottom line will come anyway.'

You might feel inhibited by the fact that you have no business background, but I firmly believe entrepreneurs are born, not made. So does Anita Roddick who founded the highly successful Body Shop International.

'I don't believe you have to be good at "business" – if you define that as the science of finance – in order to run a business successfully. The trouble is these days, people do see business as high finance. But to me, it's about trade, about buying and selling, regardless of whether it's on a market stall, or in a shop or the floor of the Stock Exchange. If I was numerate, I would never even have got to first base! But you don't have to be – you can get accountants to do all that side of it for you. I actually think it's better *not* to have a business background. If you have had a structured training, you are probably frightened to take risks, and want to do everything in the usual set routines. And without risk-taking, without breaking the rules, there would be no entrepreneurship in this country.'

Spotting the opening

Then of course you need a good idea, and there's no doubt that the best ideas come not from sitting round a table but from keeping your ears open and discovering a need. In my own case, I had been thinking for some time about what I might do next. I'd been a successful model since I was fifteen and it is such an exciting, speedy sort of life – never knowing where you're going to be from one day to the next, seeing the world on expenses, meeting interesting people – that there was no way I could simply give up once I was 'over the top' without having found a new career.

Those of us models who were over thirty spent many hours in dressing rooms, talking about what we might do next. People I worked for often complained that the younger models were appallingly unprofessional, turning up to photographic sessions with unwashed hair, no accessories etc., so together with Eve Pollard (then a fashion editor, now editor of the *Sunday Mirror*) I was seriously thinking of opening a model agency and training girls in the same way as I'd been trained by Sheelah Wilson in Manchester.

I had also been going to classes at the Dance Centre in Covent Garden for years. They had been very important to me, keeping me slim as well as sane, but the place was very overcrowded and the facilities were pretty poor. So I had started thinking about setting up something similar – obviously there was a huge demand and in many ways it seemed a very easy business. It is basically a space-letting operation – all the teachers are self-employed and simply rent studio space from you. As most people in business will tell you, finding and keeping good staff is one of the biggest problems they face, so a business that is almost staff-free seemed ideal!

The opportunity to develop this idea came towards the end of 1978, when all the teachers were told out of the blue one Monday morning, that the Dance Centre was closing down that Friday. It had been open fifteen years and suddenly all the teachers and all the professional dancers in London found themselves out on the street, not to mention hundreds of women like me for whom classes had become a vital part of their lives.

Some of the young dancers started a petition to keep it open and I became involved. We'd soon collected over two thousand names and addresses of dancers, both amateur and professional. During this time I also collected names and telephone numbers of all the teachers, telling them I would keep in touch as I was going to look for new studio space. Once the Dance Centre closed, there was no reason why someone else couldn't start up a similar venture, and with a list of over two thousand potential clients, I knew I had to do it. If I'd known then what I know now, perhaps I wouldn't even have started, but in this instance ignorance was bliss!

Anita Roddick decided to open her first Body Shop in Brighton ten years ago for a variety of reasons. For a start, she had to find something she could do to pay the bills *and* fit in with bringing up her two children then aged six and four while her husband, Gordon, took time out to ride a horse across South America.

'I then had to look at what I could do. I knew I had an up-front, showy quality – when Gordon and I ran a restaurant, we started with him out front and me in the kitchen, but within two weeks I was dying of boredom, so we swapped, and I enjoyed creating an atmosphere and dealing with people. So some kind of shop seemed a possibility. I do have a sponge-like mind and when I'd travelled to places like Madagascar and the Polynesian islands about eight years before, I'd been fascinated by what people used to cleanse or protect their skins, and it all had gone in and been stored in my brain somewhere.

'The catalyst was walking down Littlehampton High Street one day with the kids. We went into the greengrocers and bought a couple of pounds of apples and five pounds of spuds, then we went into the sweet shop and bought a quarter of this and two ounces of that, and then we went into Boots, and there was no choice of sizes. You couldn't have an ounce of this or eight ounces of that, and I thought "Why not?".

'Now, if I'd had a business background, I'd have said, "Well, I can't possibly do this because I know nothing about retailing and I know nothing about cosmetics" and that would have been that.

'You don't pull ideas out of the air. What you've got to do is find something that really really makes you angry because very often that's where there's a hole in the market. I can't understand why there isn't a company offering a bagging-up service in all supermarkets. Most supermarkets don't provide it themselves and it drives me mad. Equally, I can't understand why someone isn't importing fresh basil all year round – another hole in the market.'

Anita also believes that while you need a good idea for a business, it doesn't have to be an original idea. What you have to do, though, is put your own individual stamp on it, so that it is different and sets you apart from the competition, or simply make sure you are better:

'Suppose you're going into the hire car business – what's going to make you different? Maybe all your drivers are smartly dressed women. Maybe you put all the quality daily papers in the back of the car. Maybe you have car 'phones . . .'

In 1982, Sophie Mirman searched all over London one day for a pair of cream woolly tights to go with a particular dress and couldn't find any:

'I trekked around every hosiery department in the West End, and I realized that an everyday necessity was being sold in a difficult environment and that socks and tights should be as easy to buy as newspapers.'

Sophie started her career in Marks and Spencer's typing pool, quickly working her way up to become the secretary to Lord Sieff, the Chairman, at nineteen:

'It was the most fabulous training I could have had. Lord Sieff taught me a tremendous amount about how to get the best out of people and basically, how to do business.'

A few years later, he put her in charge of £8 million's worth of Marks and Spencer's food business until, at twenty-six, she was headhunted by the people who were setting up the Tie Rack chain and looking for a retail manager. Within six weeks, she was promoted to managing director. It was there that she met her husband, Richard Ross, and between them, they built the business up from nothing to fifteen shops in eighteen months. It turned out to be ideal training for their own venture, the potential of which was even greater, since men and women both need hosiery, and ties don't go into holes or ladders and so don't have to be replaced regularly.

Christina Smith now owns half of Covent Garden it seems. Her own enterprises include The Tea House, Neal Street East, Smith's restaurant, Café Casbar, the Flowersmith and The Postcard Gallery, not to mention all the buildings she owns in which other people have businesses. She started her career in retailing in 1957, as Terence Conran's assistant in his pre-Habitat days:

'It was at a time when things were hard – seriously hard. I did all the jobs no-one else wanted to do, from sweeping the floors to collecting money owed so that we could pay the wages at the end of the week. It was an excellent grounding in business.'

In 1962, Christina started her import business almost by accident.

'I was thinking about joining Habitat, which Terence was about to start, but there was a year to wait so I decided to go round the world. While I was travelling in countries like Mexico, Japan and Burma, I was sending samples of ethnic items back, thinking that most of it could be sold to the new Habitat. When I got back to this country, I decided with my partner at the time, David Bishop, to do it independently, and so we set up Goods and Chattels as an import business. And the new Habitat was one of our first customers.'

Ann Levick, Managing Director of Panmed Ltd, was working as a nurse in a burns unit in Salisbury, and saw how the use of pressure garments, made from a special type of elastic fabric, could dramatically reduce the scarring and the need for corrective surgery that is often the result of serious burns. But the only supplier was in America, the price was high and the delay in receiving the garments reduced considerably the good they could do. So in 1978, she took on four seamstresses who worked at home to make the garments for patients in her unit. Six months later, as word spread, the demand was so great that she had to give up nursing to concentrate on her business full time:

'I knew nothing about business – about finance and selling – so I've had to pick it up as I went along. But I do think nursing was terrific training for running a business. You learn all the people skills, you work very hard in a disciplined environment and learn not to procrastinate. You're trained to take in a situation very quickly and make a decision!'

Carol Reeves found from talking to a number of women friends who travelled to London on business regularly that what they would really like was a hotel for women only. Reeves', on Shepherd's Bush Green, opened its doors late in 1988.

Irene Mcbarek of the Pudding Club, found herself bringing up a baby single-handed after her marriage ended, and needed to make a living. Since she was a talented amateur cook, whose speciality was rich, cream-filled gateaux and puddings, she decided to put that talent to work. Commissions from friends led to other private commissions, then to an order to supply a group of casinos every day and, eventually, exclusive hotels and restaurants all round London.

In the case of Pippa Gee of Chambers International Products, it was her father who pointed out the gap in the market:

'I had been an administrator in the academic world,

working abroad, but when I met my husband who's a lawyer working locally, and decided to settle here, I had to find something to do. My father had a business selling timber and laminates – Formica and so on – and said that there was a market in this country for importing laminates from countries like France, West Germany and Italy, which are stronger on design and colour than the British ones and competitive on price. So I decided I'd set up an import business. As I had no experience of either laminates or selling, I had to find someone who did, and was very lucky to find someone with a background in both. He looked after that side of the business and I did all the admin.'

As these examples show, all of us have very different backgrounds and work experiences, but what matters is the ability to make best use of those experiences, to recognize your own strengths – and weaknesses – and build on them.

Location, location, location

There's an old saying that the three most important factors in choosing property are location, location and location. When you're deciding on a site for your business, you have to decide on what best suits your particular needs. If you're planning on opening a shop that relies on a lot of passing trade, then you want the best high street location you can afford.

In my case, I knew Covent Garden was the right area – for one thing it was close to theatres and the Opera House, and dancers were already used to coming into the area. For another, since the fruit and vegetable market had moved out, there were warehouses with the right sort of space available to let, and although the process of gentrification had begun, it still had a long way to go, so rents were still comparatively low. By chance, a photographer I knew was about to take over the lease of a derelict warehouse in Covent Garden, although he only wanted one floor. When the Dance Centre closed, I rang and asked whether he'd done the deal. He said he had – he was taking the first floor, so the basement, ground floor and second floor were vacant. I went and looked at this derelict pineapple warehouse that was full of dead pigeons and felt instinctively that, despite its appalling state, its potential was enormous, so I decided to take the ground floor and the basement – about 7000 square feet. This was the minimum I needed – 10,000 would have been better but as they needed the first floor as a photographic studio, I went ahead anyway.

Because she wanted as many people passing her shop as possible, Sophie Mirman made the decision to open the first Sock Shop in Knightsbridge tube station. It proved so successful that, subsequently, she opened many others in both tube and main line stations.

Prime site

But if you want to be in a prime site then you must have a business that will be lucrative enough to pay for it. At the Sloane Square end of the King's Road, for instance, you can expect to pay a large premium of several hundred thousand pounds and then a huge annual rent, so you have to be certain of taking a lot of money before you consider opening somewhere like that. Further down the King's Road, towards World's End, where we opened one of our pilot fashion shops in October 1987, we paid no premium and the rent was only £20,000. The position suited us very well because we were between other shops that were also catering to stylish young fashion, such as Robot, Steven King, American Classics and Vivienne Westwood's shop, so potential Pineapple customers were coming to our section of the King's Road anyway.

If you plan to open a shop serving a specialist need you can afford to be in a secondary, less expensive site. As yours is the only shop of its kind in the area, customers will seek you out wherever you are.

If you're manufacturing specialist equipment for a small number of firms all over the country, then a workshop near the M25 with easy access to all the other motorways would be ideal. If you have the sort of business that involves keeping a lot of stock in warehouses, there's no reason why they should all be together. When the first warehouse the Sock Shop rented in London was beginning to bulge at the seams, Sophie Mirman decided to rent another one in the Midlands to hold longer-term stock. Once Sock Shops started opening all over the British Isles and no longer just in the south east, it made sense to have warehousing located centrally in the country. And of course, rents on commercial property are much lower outside London.

If you are running a telephone business or a consultancy that involves visiting clients rather than them coming to you, there's no reason why you can't base yourself, initially anyway, in the spare bedroom at home. Obviously, if clients are going to visit you, then you must have premises that look professional, but remember in most businesses, offices don't make money!

When you start to look for premises, you should not only put your name on the list of all the local estate agents, but also look at the business property columns in the local paper and walk the streets yourself. I learnt this lesson when I was buying a house – I found exactly what I was looking for in the paper, although this particular house was with an estate agent on whose mailing list I'd been for months!

If you see the premises you fancy, there's nothing to be lost by going in and asking if the owner or tenant feels like moving. You never know, they may have been thinking about it, and someone offering a good price may be the deciding factor.

Making do

When we opened in Covent Garden, my office was at home. I then moved into what was basically a very large cupboard with all the electricity meters. One day, a man from the LEB came, threw us out, put a large lock on the door and a 'No Entry' sign. Quite inadvertently, we had been breaking the law! When I finally did get an office, I shared it with about seven other people. It was also right next to the studios, so I would have a piano playing from Maryon Lane's ballet class through one partition wall, and Charles Augins's bongo drums through another! And it was very accessible to all the dancers. We were trying to get the book-keeping done on one occasion, when Wayne Sleep appeared in the office as he often did. We said 'Oh hi, Wayne' and just carried on with the books. Next thing we knew Wayne had stripped off to his jockstrap, jumped onto the desk top and was doing pirouettes – a sure way of getting our undivided attention! Unfortunately I had to move my office some time later as it was almost impossible to get any work done! But I really miss those early days. It was so exciting and such fun, and after all, that was the reason I was doing it!

MARKET RESEARCH

Obviously you need to know a little bit about the area. If you're thinking of opening a shop or restaurant, once you have found premises you like the look of, visit the street at different times of the day and of the week. It may be busy in the daytime, but completely deserted in the evening and on Sundays, which is fine if you want to open a shop, but not so good for a fast-food restaurant.

Check out parking – if there are double yellow lines stretching into the distance in all directions and no car park handy, you can't rely on customers in cars. Check out the traffic flow. Are there traffic lights nearby so motorists can see the shop as they wait for the lights to turn green, or is it just round a bend so they can't see it until they're almost past? If there's a central barrier with no gaps for a couple of miles, they are unlikely to come all the way back just to see you.

Planning permission

You must check on planning permission. You may plan to carry on exactly the same sort of business as the existing occupier, but you'd be very unwise to assume that she has been granted the necessary planning permission or that the permission automatically carries on if the business changes hands. If she hasn't, or it doesn't, then your business could be closed down or you could be forced to revert to its original use – a garage, say, when you thought you were taking over a health food restaurant.

If you plan to start a different type of business you must also check the position relating to change of use with the local authority. In our case, the planning department was quite happy for us to change the use of the building, even though 'warehouse' to 'dance centre' was a big change. The character of the whole area was undergoing a radical change and it was extremely unlikely that any pineapple merchant would ever want to rent it again.

It is well worth contacting the local Chamber of Commerce, and telling them your plans. If there are already enough health clubs or wine bars in the town, then they may well oppose your application for a change of use, and succeed. Prepare your case well before you make your application and, as I found out, it is better to apply in person.

Freehold, leasehold or stranglehold?

The question of whether freehold or leasehold premises are better is to a large extent answered by your financial circumstances. Personally, I prefer freeholds, I like bricks and mortar, probably as a result of my northern upbringing! When I started Pineapple New York we bought the premises freehold. But as the late Allen Foster of B&Q said to me, 'You're not in the property business, and buying freehold means that you have money tied up in property that you could be using to develop your business.'

In my own defence let me say that New York was a special case because if you take out a lease there, once it has expired your landlord can, in certain circumstances, move in and take over the running of your business. And it was certainly a very sound investment. In four years the property almost tripled in value.

If you are taking over a leasehold property, there are a number of questions you must ask – how long has the lease got to run, is it renewable, is there a rent-free period and how much needs spending on the building? Obviously if the lease is only five years, isn't renewable and the building needs a fortune spending on it, it isn't a sound commercial proposition. Or so it would seem. From 1963 onwards when Christina Smith took over an old potato store (now The Neal Street Restaurant), in the heart of the then still-thriving Covent Garden fruit and vegetable market, she bought up lots of short-term leases in the area simply because 'it seemed like a good idea at the time.' Among them was a warehouse at Seven Dials which was due for demolition under redevelopment plans. Christina converted it for mixed commercial and community use, and as a 'nursery' for small, new businesses. In 1980 the decision to demolish the building was reversed, and she was offered a sixty-five year lease instead of the six-month lease she then had!

Before you even think about signing a lease, get an experienced lawyer, specializing in commercial property, to go through it with a fine-tooth comb.

Once you have found premises and a lease that are sound, you must expect to pay 'key money' (a lump sum to the existing leaseholder) if they are empty, or a premium if the existing business is still trading. You can expect to pay between thirty and forty-five weeks' average takings. There are no premiums on new property or leases, though if you decide to move on and sell the remainder of your lease, then you can charge a premium. In fact these days, it's a very good way to make money! Very often you will be expected to give personal guarantees on a lease – a factor that puts most people off before they have even started, but what you need here is faith in yourself and your vision.

Outgrowing the garden shed

If you are planning to set up a manufacturing business, it might be possible to start off in the garage or shed at home, though if the process is noisy or smelly, or involves a steady stream of callers, then the neighbours and the local authority will soon register their protests. Even if what you're making – curtains, say, or soft toys – isn't likely to draw the authorities' attention, you must still inform your insurance company about your activities or you may well find that you have inadvertently invalidated your household policies.

If your business starts to grow, you'll soon find you need bigger premises, and it has never been easier for small businesses to find them. All over the country, enterprise centres are opening up, some in derelict factories, others purpose built, offering small units to rent. The benefits of these centres are that as your business grows, you can often increase the space you rent, and they also offer valuable shared services such as telephone answering, secretarial services and even business advice, which you simply wouldn't be able to afford on your own. The Industrial Development Officer at the local town hall should be able to tell you what's available in your area.

If you only need office space for your business, then initially working from home is a good idea because obviously your overheads will be very low. There are drawbacks, though. Family and friends find it hard to accept that you're working, and potential clients will not be too impressed if your telephone calls are interrupted with the background noises of babies crying!

STREET CRED

Equally, it's harder to establish credibility if your business address is '27, Railway Cuttings'. It would be well worth your while to investigate the nearest Business Centre. (Look in Yellow Pages under 'Office Rental'.) They are opening up in many towns and cities, and offer a whole range of services to small businesses, from telephone answering and forwarding mail, to word processing and fax machines. In many cases they will rent you office space by the hour, if that's all you need, and if you need to impress a client, some will even provide coffee or lunch.

ESTIMATING YOUR GROWTH

It's very hard to gauge, especially if you are fairly new in business, just how big your premises should be. Obviously you don't want to spend more than you have to on somewhere that's too big for your needs. Equally, you don't want all the upheaval of moving into somewhere that's only just big enough and then have to go through it all again a year or so later.

I remember having lunch with Sophie Mirman at the Sock Shop warehouse they had just taken over, and thinking it was like an aircraft hangar. Sophie, too, wondered if she had made a terrible mistake:

'There were just two tiers of stock in one corner and the rest of the warehouse stretched into the distance like a football pitch. I was convinced we'd have to sublet half of it. But now, two years later, it's full right up to the ceiling, and some days we have boxes piling up outside waiting for a space!'

It really is a question of making an educated guess, erring perhaps on the side of optimism. If your premises are too large then you can always sublet part of them if your lease allows.

TIME IS MONEY

Once you have signed your lease, then you have to get moving fast. You're paying money out – rent, rates, utilities – but until you start trading, you're getting nothing back. It may mean you have to open sooner than you'd like – we opened at Covent Garden with no loos and a cement mixer still in reception – but in most cases that's the lesser of two evils. This time factor is something you must take into account when you start to work out how much money you will need to raise.

Obtaining the finance

If the business you propose to start is a consultancy involving just you and a telephone initially, or a small-scale catering business that you can run from home, then obviously you don't need to borrow any money to get started. But if your business involves buying or renting premises and buying equipment or stock, then unless you have some rich-and-kind-relations, you will need to raise the necessary finance.

NOW GET A GOOD ACCOUNTANT

The most likely source of a loan to start your business is your local high street bank, but before you even telephone the manager for an appointment, you must get yourself a good accountant. You can't simply approach the bank manager with a good idea, you have to be able to present him with a proper business plan – with your costings, forecasts, cash flows and so on – and the accountant will show you the format. The best way to find a good accountant, and indeed any pro-fessional adviser, is to ask around. Ask friends with small businesses. If someone you trust recommends an accountant whom they have used successfully for some years, then he, or she, is almost certainly a good bet.

THE BUSINESS PLAN

While your accountant will show you how to draw up a business plan, he won't tell you the figures to write down. You have to do that yourself. You will know how much your premises are going to cost you – not just rent and rates, but other fixed costs such as insurance, heating, lighting, telephone – and how much your equipment or stock will cost. And then you have to make an educated guess at how much money you can take in a day. With Pineapple, I was lucky because I was able to calculate from the signatures on the petition we organized when the Dance Centre closed down, the number of teachers and potential members there were. It wasn't difficult to work out and in fact I was spot on with the first year's forecast.

When I was preparing the forecasts for the shop, which was much more of an unknown factor, I just went through a day in my mind, imagining how many people might come in and what sort of things they might buy. Seasonal factors have to be taken into account – August is usually pretty flat, for example, because so many people are on holiday; Christmas is busier than normal. By doing this you can work out your average daily, weekly and monthly sales. Be as realistic as you can. It might even be worth doing two forecasts – one optimistic, one pessimistic – and splitting the difference.

When you've done all the sums, don't look at the amount you need to borrow and think 'Oh, that's far too much. I'll knock off a few thousand'. So many small business fail because they are under-capitalized. If that's what the business you are planning will cost to get started, that's what it will cost. If it's clear from your plan that the business won't be making enough to cover the repayments, then you must think again. Maybe you should think about cheaper premises, leasing equipment or even buying it second-hand. We bought all our office furniture at the local auction house, and we even got a partition wall second-hand. The district surveyor mentioned that someone was throwing it out, so we got it very cheaply! Certainly if the figures don't make sense before you even start, you are heading for disaster. It's also a good idea at this point to have in your mind a figure that you are prepared to lose as you must be willing to recognize the risk at this stage.

THE LISTENING FRIENDLY BANK MANAGER IN THE CUPBOARD

When I was ready to present my plan late in 1978, I heard that banks in the Covent Garden area were being encouraged to lend money to new businesses starting up in the area after the fruit market had been relocated, so naturally I approached a Covent Garden bank manager. He was very enthusiastic and I think what impressed him most was the copy of the petition I showed him with the names and addresses of two thousand potential customers with nowhere else to go as well as a list of over fifty top teachers desperate for studio space!

Of course your figures have to stack up and you have to present them professionally, but the bank manager will also be assessing you as a person. He knows that what makes businesses succeed are people, so they want to see that you are committed, enthusiastic, energetic and on top of it all. The bank manager and your accountant should advise you on the various government schemes that can assist you, for example, the Enterprise Initiative Scheme and the government Loan Guarantee Scheme.

ASSESS YOUR IMAGE

It's important that you look right. I'm often quoted as saying you don't have to conform. That's true – you don't have to adopt a uniform – but you must look as though you're together and neat. You want to be comfortable in what you're wearing in order to look relaxed and confident, so avoid clothes that need fiddling with, such as wrap-over skirts or elaborate collars. I would also avoid low necklines, very short skirts, lots of make-up and too much jewellery. Tip your handbag out before you go and get rid of inessential clutter. If you do happen to drop it, crumpled lipstick-stained tissues, old shopping lists and till receipts spilling out will not create the right impression!

While you should be comfortable, you obviously can't be too casual, as Anita Roddick found out:

'When I first approached the bank manager about a £4,000 loan to start the first Body Shop in 1976, I didn't have a clue about how to act. Then, twelve years ago, there were no magazine articles telling you about things like that. So I went dressed in jeans and an old Bob Dylan T-shirt, with my daughter Samantha on my back in a papoose and Justine in the pushchair, and started telling him about this great idea I'd had and how wonderful it was going to be . . .

'Zilch! He wasn't going to lend me a penny. I went

home, told Gordon and he said, "He wants us to act in a conventional way, so that's what we'll do. You go out and buy a pinstriped suit, we'll put our piece of paper in plastic folders, I'll come with you and we'll give him what he wants." That's what we did and we got the loan immediately.'

Anita's response to the view that women shouldn't have to jump through hoops in order to get what they want is typically down-to-earth:

'B*llsh*t! To get what you want, the intelligent thing to do is to adapt. Then, when you've got what you want, the intelligent thing is not to dilute your image!'

FAMILY COMMITMENTS

If you have a family, you must expect the bank manager to ask about your child-care arrangements and you have to convince him that this side of your life is well-organized even if it isn't. No, of course they wouldn't ask a man the same question, but not only must you not resent it, you must also accept that, as a woman with a family wanting to start a business, you are at a disadvantage. We are catching up, but not as fast as we should. What you have to do is convince him that even with a home and family to run, you are still worth backing.

Of course there is still some discrimination against women, but it is dying out. Jean Bradley, manager of a branch of Lloyds Bank in the City, believes that with younger managers there is very little discrimination and they judge a project purely on its merits.

'What does sometimes happen is that if a woman's request for a business loan is turned down because the manager doesn't believe it is sound, she will assume it's because she's a woman. And it's also true that when it comes to the crunch and businesswomen are asked to put the family home on the line as security for the business borrowing facility, they are less willing to take that risk than men.'

Putting the house up as security for the loan was something I had to do, and to be honest, it didn't bother me that much. I passionately wanted to get my business off the ground, and the fear of failure would never have stopped me taking the risk of starting out on my own.

If your bank manager turns you down, or you don't get on with him, try somewhere else. The important thing to remember is that money is a commodity you pay for through bank charges and interest, so bank managers are there to work for you, not to make your life more difficult.

Sharing the business

If you can't get any bank to lend you the money, you might be tempted to take on a partner, giving them a share of the business in return for capital. My advice would be to resist the temptation if you possibly can. I don't think it's a good idea to have a partner in business anyway. It's great to get the input from other people but at the end of the day, you want to be the one who makes the decisions.

With a partner you have to discuss all the issues and everything takes twice as long. A discussion can soon turn into an argument and partners can so easily fall out. If you do decide to take a partner, a sleeping partner is probably best and you must ask your lawyer to draw up a shareholders' agreement before you start. As any lawyer will tell you it's much more difficult to end a business partnership than a marriage!

I personally think it's much better to build a team around you – have weekly management meetings with time for discussion and communication. (Creativity does rub off and energy breeds energy!) But at the end of the day one person has to take the final responsibility.

Christina Smith who started her business with a partner isn't so sure that it is a bad idea:

'After a while, my partner felt the business was moving in a direction he didn't like – he wanted to make more things here and was especialy interested in textiles – and so he went off to do his own thing. I hadn't been aware of any problems or friction and hadn't found it difficult to work with him, though he obviously found it difficult to work with me.

'I do miss having a partner in many ways, not having anyone to talk to about the business, not having anyone who's been through the difficult times.'

If you're thinking about giving someone a share of your business in order to raise capital, you must think very hard not just about what happens if the business fails, but what happens if it succeeds.

In 1977 when Anita Roddick couldn't raise the money from the bank to open her second Body Shop, she sold a half-share in the business to a local businessman for £4,000. Seven years later, when the company went public, he collected £2 million for just a small slice of his shares! As she says now, it was a big mistake:

'If you have an idea which is good, never dilute your

interest by selling off part of it, or getting someone in to keep you company. If you need to borrow, borrow. Don't give yourself away. Have the courage to know you will be a success!'

While that's true, if it really was the only way Anita could raise the money to expand, then it's better to have only half of a multi-million pound empire than one hundred per cent of one small shop in Brighton!

Sophie Mirman and her husband, Richard Ross, were luckier. In spite of their backgrounds – retailing and accountancy respectively – and the fact that they had a proven success with a very similar type of business, the Tie Rack chain, they found it extremely difficult to raise the start-up capital for their first Sock Shop in Knightsbridge underground station, which opened in April 1983. They offered 49% of their business to a venture capitalist in return for £45,000 but fortunately he turned them down. After the company went public in April 1987, and even after the Crash the following autumn, that stake would have been worth about £15 million!

Eventually they raised the money through the government's Loan Guarantee Scheme, in which the government guarantees up to 80% of approved bank loans up to £85,000, in exchange for a 2.5% premium, over and above the bank's interest rate, on the actual sum guaranteed.

Making the dream concrete

If you're lucky, once your finances have been arranged you can move into your new premises and get started. We weren't so lucky. What we took over was the ground floor and basement of a derelict warehouse. The process of turning such a building into a public place, with all the rules and regulations, is an absolutely huge undertaking. Had I known beforehand how huge, I might well not have had the nerve to tackle it.

Because I had very little money to play with, I couldn't afford an architect or a building contractor so I had to wear both hats. I drew up the plans myself, though I still don't know how I knew what to do. I suppose I looked at other plans, and then looked at the building. A certain amount is just common-sense. We had to get in as many good-sized studios as we could and they had to be where the high ceilings were. And then you have to have certain corridors and exits because of fire regulations, which the fire officer tells you all about.

Since I was my own building contractor, I took on the builders, electricians, plumbers and so on. It really was a nightmare, trying to orchestrate the whole thing, getting the right people to come at the right time so that, for example, the plasterer came after the electrician had finished making holes in the walls and not before.

We had to get rid of the first lot of builders, because they were absolute cowboys, and I even ended up in court as one of them forged my signature on a cheque for £2,000! Most people have problems with builders and its very difficult to find good ones. Once you do, you need to hang on to them. My second lot – managed by Pete 'Sparks' – were terrific and have worked on all our building projects over the years. I used to go home very late at night covered in brick dust and be back at 7 a.m. the next morning in case they needed anything. If they suddenly ran out of 10-inch nails, it was much better for me to jump in the car to go and get them than for them to down tools.

NO TIME TO WASTE

Not only were we on a tight budget, we were also working against the clock. When the Dance Centre closed down, I wasn't the only person who saw the opportunity which had presented itself, so there was a race to be the first to open. Whoever won would get the best teachers, and they were the key to success. So all the time we were working on Pineapple, I kept in touch with the teachers, showing them the plans, keeping them warm as it were. They were all very helpful and enthusiastic, fortunately, for without the teachers I had no business.

Early one Saturday morning when we had already spent a fortune but the studios were only half built, a teacher rang to tell me the Dance Centre was about to re-open, having been completely refurbished.

All the teachers had been invited back by this unexpected competition. I held my breath but one by one they rang that day to assure me they would wait for Pineapple. They felt that as they had been so badly treated they wouldn't go back. In fact only a couple of teachers did go back, and as a result the Dance Centre had to move away from dance into fitness.

During this time I kept up my much needed dance classes. The teachers were scattered around various church halls and I went to John Gordon's class. He'd found a rather dubious basement below a strip club in Soho! This kept up my stamina level and my sanity! John's encouragement (not to mention desperation for his new studio at Pineapple!) also helped to keep me going.

MAKE A NUISANCE OF YOURSELF!

As I said, the problems involved in converting a ware-house into a public place were enormous, not just in the sheer practicalities, but in complying with all the rules and regulations. Due to my persistence we were granted planning permission very quickly – it usually takes at least six months to go through and of course you can't move without it. And once you've started, the work has to be inspected by health inspectors (who held us up more than anyone else – drains need more inspection that I would have dreamed possible!), fire inspectors and district surveyors. They have loads of buildings to visit so if you have to wait for them to visit yours before you can carry on, that can also slow you down. What I did was to make a thorough nuisance of myself, calling in to see them, nagging and cajoling until they thought, 'Oh let's get this job out of the way. This woman is driving us mad!' In fact we were very lucky in this respect and I can't help feeling it was more than just coincidence that one man we had to deal with was called Mr Dance!

DON'T GIVE UP NOW!

About half-way through the building work, it was suddenly decided that, since buildings over a certain number of cubic feet have to be concrete if the general public are going to use them, and since our building was over that size, and it was a wooden framed building, it wasn't suitable for a dance studio!

Frantic, I rang various fireproofing firms and asked how you can make a wooden building like a concrete one. In the end, the floors, ceilings and walls had to be lined and even the steel pillars had to be clad with a fireproof material. It was a major construction job, but it was acceptable. When the district surveyor came to see it I couldn't resist asking if he wanted me to clad my desk. It was wood after all!

At one point I employed an architect to design a mezzanine floor for the reception area. You must keep an eye on everybody and everything. I made the mistake of assuming that he knew what he was doing but unfortunately the day before we were due to open the district surveyor put a closure order on the building as the mezzanine was an unsafe structure for public use. All I could do was promise to pull it down overnight. He promised to be back at 9 a.m.! So my builders worked all night to take the structure down – it meant the loss of £1,000 worth of timber, not to mention the labour. But it came down a lot faster than it went up! The district surveyor kept his promise and arrived at 9 a.m. the next morning and declared us officially open.

To be fair, I found that most officials were very helpful, and happy to offer the benefit of their experience. Just before we were due to open, we fell foul of the steel strike, so the fire escape couldn't be built in time for us to open on schedule. The fire officer said, 'You can't open on time, and that's that.' But refusing to take no for an answer as usual, I said there had to be a way round it. He said, 'Well, you can have temporary fire escapes built with scaffolding.' I asked if he could recommend a firm, but he said he wasn't allowed to; indeed he'd said too much already. So I got out the Yellow Pages and dialled a few scaffolding companies. Eventually I found one who did build approved temporary fire escapes, and who could do it within the necessary timescale.

Don't ever think that because you've survived something terrible you can relax – there are always more problems around the corner when you're in business. We had a positive nightmare with our telephones – after weeks of promises and broken appointments and a week before we were due to open, the GPO (as it was then) calmly told us we wouldn't have our telephones in time after all and would have to wait several months. I couldn't believe it. The telephone is crucial for survival in any business and it was the first thing I'd applied for six months earlier. In desperation I joined the Chamber of Commerce who immediately solved the problem and have been increasingly helpful over the years.

So we did open on time – six months after we'd started – and the dancers were so thrilled to have somewhere to come after so long that they didn't mind at all that there was still a cement mixer in reception, or that they had to use the loos in pubs and other buildings nearby! The Film School next door was particularly helpful and Betty Feldman who ran it was very kind, allowing scantily-clad dancers to trail in and out all day for several weeks!

YELLOW PAGES

In the early days, if I couldn't find the people I needed through friends and acquaintances, I used Yellow

Pages. Anita Roddick did too. Once she had finally got her bank loan, she estimated she had £700 to spend on products. So she rang two major cosmetics manufacturers, and didn't know whether they were more amused by the minuscule quantities she was asking for, or the weird ingredients she wanted to use – aloe vera, cocoa butter, jojoba oil and so on. Having got nowhere with them, she turned to Yellow Pages and under 'H' for Herbalists she found a member of the Herbal Society who was having difficulty selling his products 'because they were too honest', and who was willing to help. Their first batch of products was made up in the Roddicks' kitchen, and that man's company has grown alongside the Body Shop International. Anita is delighted and eternally grateful to him. 'That company gave me a chance.'

DON'T RELY ON EXPERTS!

I learnt a number of valuable lessons during that six months, not least of which was not to be intimidated by 'experts'. As I have said, never assume that they know what they're doing. To have the mirrors in the studios fitted, I brought in a company that specialized in glazing who'd been doing that sort of thing for years. Perhaps I should have heard warning bells when they asked me how I wanted the mirrors put on the wall! I said, patiently, that I didn't know. I had assumed they would tell me. In the end, they screwed them into the wall and the mirrors cracked between the screw holes. Thousands of pounds worth of mirrors later, it turned out that they should have been stuck onto boards and then mounted on the wall. We also learnt that mirrors which are fixed flat on the wall make you look fat, so they need tilting slightly to give you a longer look. That was a very expensive lesson.

IMPROVISE

When it came to the floors, which have to be sprung, I got a number of companies in to tell me how to do it. But floors are very expensive to put in and a nightmare to maintain because the resin from the dancers' shoes gets into them so they have to be scrubbed, but then they get too slippery . . . Eventually I came up with a way of doing the floors that was much cheaper and much easier to maintain. I discovered in New York that some dance studios were using a new floor covering and that a firm in this country was about to produce something similar. We couldn't just lay that down because the floors had to be sprung, so I got a carpenter to put down some slats of wood with some boarding on top which we then covered in the new covering. And it worked brilliantly. I got Wayne Sleep to test it for me, and he gave it his seal of approval.

A lot of brilliant ideas stem from pure necessity. Anita Roddick's decision to have cheap plastic bottles and handwritten labels was due to the fact that she couldn't afford anything else. Now ten years on, it means that the Body Shop International can be extremely flexible and fast in introducing new products. While the cosmetic giants are spending a year designing the container and the packaging for a new product, the Body Shop International can simply put it in the usual bottles, get the labels hand-written and have it on the shelves in weeks. If it's not a success, then they're not left with a warehouseful of redundant and very costly containers and boxes.

A pineapple by any other name

What you choose to call your company is also important, and often the simplest ideas are the best. Think of the Sock Shop, the Body Shop – they tell immediately what the business is, and they are easy to remember. In my case, since the building had been a pineapple warehouse I thought 'Pineapple' would be perfect, not least because it's so easy to remember. So Pineapple Dance Studios it became. I remember Laverne Meyer, one of our ballet teachers, taking me out to tea and saying, 'My dear, you can't call it that! It sounds so commercial! You should call it the "Covent Garden Academy of Dance".'

I said, 'This place has cost such a lot of money that people have got to remember its name. It has to be commercial for us to survive. For professional dancers to have somewhere to dance, we have to have the general public bringing in enough money to make it work.'

If yours is a jokey sort of business then a jokey name is fine, but otherwise resist the temptation. Jokes wear thin very quickly, and you can hardly expect potential customers to take your company seriously if you appear not to do so. That said, though, a successful business can survive almost anything. Look at Virgin Records. By the time the name 'Virgin' came to be emblazoned across a Boeing 747, we were all so used to it that nobody batted an eyelid.

Look professional

While there are certain things you can afford to save money on – office furniture and so on – there are other areas where cutting corners would be a false economy. Your stationery, for example, must look professional. Get it printed – there are quick print shops in most towns now and they don't charge a fortune. Whatever you do, don't get one of those stamps made with the company's name and address on and use it on ordinary writing paper.

Although we didn't know it at the time we opened Pineapple Covent Garden, design and image would become one of our major strengths as the company grew and developed. I knew nothing about graphics, but just knew I wanted the name written like the Ritz Hotel – early 1940s style. Women are more instinctive than men, and you must just open up your mind and be prepared to back your instincts. You must never say 'I haven't done this before so I can't do it!'

My next door neighbour at the time was Ian Logan, a designer, so I talked to him about it. He suggested the lady with the pineapple. In fact in the original 1940s picture, she was holding a beach ball, but we substituted the pineapple. The colours we chose were very pineapply too – yellowy, cream paper, with orange and brown printing with the odd green leaf here and there. We've been through many changes since then, but more of that later . . . if you don't have a visual imagination, then you can get some help from someone who does. There are lots of extremely talented – and very pricey – design groups around, but since money will be tight, why not approach the local art college?

Anita Roddick paid a student in Brighton £25 for the Body Shop's famous lotus logo!

Public relations

No matter what kind of business you start, you have to let your potential customers know you exist, otherwise you will have no business. It's very unlikely, initially, that you will be able to afford to advertise, and in any case, I believe that Public Relations is a much more effective way of spreading the word. PR isn't an extra that you can have later on when you can afford it. PR means selling, and selling is business, so what is business if it's not PR?

At the beginning, I did all the PR myself because we couldn't afford to pay anyone and besides, people would much rather talk to you than to your PR agency. I was very lucky in that I had lots of journalist contacts from my modelling days, so I could 'phone people and tell them what we were doing. And since the whole saga of the Dance Centre closing and all the dancers being out on the street had been a very good story, we got lots of media coverage in the early days.

At a party, I overheard journalist Celia Brayfield discussing the fate of the Dance Centre, so I introduced myself, and told her that we had just started the building work at Pineapple. A few days later, a story about us appeared in the Londoner's Diary in the *Evening Standard*, and their switchboard was blocked with calls from the people wanting to know when we were opening. Suddenly we were really on the map!

Jan Murray, the doyenne of dance critics, was a great

supporter of ours from the start, and her interest was invaluable in terms of the publicity it gave us. I also contacted other well-known dance critics and writers whom I didn't know personally. It's always a good idea to contact people who specialize in your type of business.

THE RIGHT MEDIA

Read through all the relevant magazines and news-papers, see what kind of stories they run, and who's doing what. If you want to get your message read, then make sure you address it to the right person. No-one likes receiving mail addressed to their predecessor who left a year ago, or having their name spelt wrong.

Anita Roddick, ever original, is a great believer in the value of the anonymous phone call. Her first Body Shop in Brighton just happened to be situated between two firms of undertakers who, understandably, objected to a business with that name opening up:

'I made a phone call to the local paper, with a handkerchief over the mouthpiece to disguise my voice, and said that there was this poor woman with two children to bring up, trying to open this natural skin product shop, who was having problems with these two firms of undertakers! It made almost a full page in the local paper!'

Even today, with Body Shop International a multi-million pound business, Anita has never paid a penny for advertising:

'The one exception was at an award ceremony recently, jointly run by a charity. We paid for a page in the programme.'

The same is true of Sock Shop and Pineapple. But we have had huge amounts of coverage in newspapers and magazines which we would never have been able to afford to pay for in a million years. And besides, editorial coverage is worth so much more to your business than advertising simply because it can't be bought. One of the few advantages women in business have is that the media love successful women!

Local papers, free sheets and magazines are always in the market for local stories, so if you can come up with an interesting angle and perhaps a photograph or two on what you're doing, they will usually be only too glad to write a story. You may find they will push you to advertise in the same issue but resist if you can. Some businesses of course have to advertise and a very good way to market your product is below the line marketing, such as T-shirts and other promotional goods. There are now lots of companies specializing in this but beware of costs and make sure you are targetting your customer! Leafleting your area is an effective way to start and not too costly.

A good grasp of basic finance

It is absolutely vital to have a good grasp of basic finance and to have a clear picture, on a monthly basis at the very least, of what the situation is. At one time people used to do only annual or six-monthly accounting, but you simply can't afford to wait that long to see what's happening – at its most basic, how much you're spending and how much is coming in.

You don't have to be good at maths, because monthly

management accounts are really quite logical and simple. Just get your accountant to explain it to you or, if you really can't afford one, then enrol for a small business course which many further education colleges run now and which will teach you the basics.

My mum is good at book-keeping, so she taught me how to keep my books when I started modelling at fifteen. It was simply a case of writing down the jobs I'd done, how many hours, and what expenses there were to be claimed for travel or accessories. When the cheque came in from the agency it was just a question of ticking it off, so I always knew how much was outstanding. I was also registered for VAT so I had to be meticulous in keeping a record, as well as receipts, so that I could claim it back.

When you're starting out, it's best to do the book-keeping yourself so that you have complete control of the money. You'll need a petty cash book, to record all the small cash purchases, and a daily cash book, in which you write down every cheque you pay out and every cheque you receive. You should always have an up-to-date picture of the situation at the bank, and know what is owing to you, and when things are likely to get tight.

'TURNOVER IS VANITY, PROFITS ARE SANITY'

You should always remember that performance is assessed on profit, not on turnover. You may hear people say that such and such a company turned over two million last year, as if that was an indication of success. What you need to know is how much they spend to get that turnover. If it was £1,999,500, then the profit is only £500 or .025% of the turnover – hardly a success story. As Mr Micawber said: 'Annual income twenty pounds, annual expenditure nineteen, nineteen and six – result happiness. Annual income twenty pounds, annual expenditure twenty pounds, nought and six – result misery.'

Increasing your overdraft

There are times in business when you need to increase your overdraft.

In autumn 1988, for example, we got some very large orders from several of the big mail order catalogues. We had to pay our manufacturers before the catalogues paid us, so that meant we would need to increase our overdraft facility for a month or so. We told the bank that this would happen in October, but the money to cover it would arrive in November, and asked if that was all right. They agreed. Don't lose an opportunity but, on the other hand, you must never assume it will be all right with the bank. Always ask, always tell them what the time scale will be, and make sure you have really covered yourself. If you ask for £50,000 and it turns out to be £100,000, it's very difficult to go back for more.

KEEP THE CASH FLOW FLOWING

There's no doubt that cash flow creates more problems for small businesses than almost anything else and since your cash flow means your profits, you can see that it is crucial to get it right.

With the studios, I have to pay the rent three months in advance, so I thought it not unreasonable to expect the teachers to pay a month in advance. A couple of them do, but most of them live from day to day and want to pay on a daily basis, which means that for the last day of each quarter they've had eighty-nine days' credit from me!

Large companies are notorious for slow payment to small ones. A recent check among some very well-known companies showed that, on average, they took eight weeks to pay up.

GET THE MONEY IN

A lot of businesses, especially when dealing with new customers, insist on cash on delivery, and that is becoming more and more widely accepted. Make sure you always send out accurate invoices. If you don't you won't hear anything from the company concerned until you send a reminder thirty days later. Then they'll say 'we haven't paid because the invoice isn't right' and that gives them another month's grace while you argue about it and sort it out.

Many large companies pay all their invoices once a month, so it's worth trying to find out when the cut-off point is. It may be the last day of the month or may be the 27th or 28th. Obviously if, by sending your invoice to them a few days earlier than you otherwise would, you get paid a month earlier, it's well worth the effort. If the money is going to be earning interest (or saving the interest on an overdraft) then it's better that it's in your account than in theirs.

You might consider offering incentives. A photographer I know adds a bit on to his bill and then offers a

10% discount to clients who settle within twenty-eight days. If it doesn't work, then the little extra he's charging helps with the overdraft!

Other than that, you just have to learn to be very good at chasing money, and not take this singularly British attitude that it's vulgar to do so. Chase people up on the 'phone – everyone in business has a cash flow problem and so they'll only pay the people who pressure them. If you still have no joy, and your cash flow has slowed to a trickle, it might be worth a solicitor's letter threatening legal action if they don't pay up. That won't cost you very much, although taking legal action can be a very costly, lengthy business. It's not that expensive to slap a writ on people who owe you money, either, though if you hope to do business with them again, that's probably not advisable.

If you have a large debt outstanding, or indeed a number of smaller ones, you could hand them over to a collection agency or factoring company who will pay you a percentage of the debt – up to 80% – right away, and the balance once they have collected it. Check on the fees before you commit yourself, as the costs can be quite high. Factoring is a more sophisticated service than just debt collecting, and having managed to shake off the notion that companies using factors had to be in serious difficulties, it's becoming more widely used all the time.

Legal problems

I don't think it's possible to be in business for any length of time and avoid litigation in one form or another. So, along with a good accountant and bank manager, you must also have a good solicitor – one experienced in the legal side of running a business. The solicitors who did the conveyancing on your house or even on your business premises may not be the right person for this particular line of work.

The chances are that you'll be on the receiving end of litigation before you instigate it yourself. Someone – a customer, a supplier – will serve a writ on you, perhaps because you have refused to replace goods they consider faulty or because you are late in paying a bill. The most important piece of advice I can give anyone in that situation is *'Don't panic'*. I know some people are absolutely terrified of anything to do with the law, whether it's policemen, the courts, or lawyers, and assume that if they receive any legal communication at all, they are automatically in the wrong and the prison gates loom. But I repeat, don't panic. Pass the writ onto your solicitor and let him deal with it – don't put it off.

Don't forget, many people use writs as a cheap and easy way of frightening debtors into paying up (indeed, I've even suggested you try it yourself). They have no intention of actually taking the case to court because it will cost them far more both in terms of money and aggravation than the outstanding debt.

Other people are simply trying it on. We hadn't even opened Pineapple New York when my first writ was served on me – in my hotel room, just as I was leaving to catch the plane home! It was from a man who had initially wanted to set up his own dance studio within

53

Pineapple, but then decided that he wanted to run the whole thing, even though I was the one coming up with the money! We couldn't agree and, naturally, with litigation being an important part of the American way of life, he tried to sue me, though without success.

In this country we are nowhere near as litigious as the Americans, yet there are people here who will also try it on. A year or so ago, we received a strong letter from a very heavyweight firm of solicitors, claiming that we had copied the design of a petticoat made by a client of theirs and demanding compensation. Of course we hadn't – our net petticoats then on sale were simply a slightly updated version of the ballet petticoats we'd been selling for years, long before they became a fashion item. I passed the letter onto our solicitor, and sent someone out to buy a petticoat made by this designer so we could show the solicitor the differences between it and ours. In fact, it wasn't possible to buy the petticoat in question – it wasn't manufactured any more – but it was possible to buy petticoats from the same designer which were very similar indeed to those that Pineapple had been selling for years. Our solicitor wrote back, stating all this and pointing out that perhaps we had a case against their client. Funnily enough, we haven't heard a word from them since.

While you really shouldn't panic when you get a writ, you shouldn't simply chuck it in the bin and forget about it either. A few years ago, we had some time-tables printed by our printers, but they were completely illegible and we had to ask for them to be done again. When our statement came in, we saw what appeared to be a duplicated item of £90 and we assumed, wrongly, that it was just an administrative error and so we only paid it once. We continued to ignore the £90 on subsequent statements. The next thing that happened was that the printers took out a Winding Up Order against us. That meant that if we didn't pay the £90 by a certain date, a hearing would be held and everyone to whom we owed money would turn up and ask to be paid. That's bad enough for a small business where cash flow is crucial, because it's just not possible to pay off your creditors until your debtors pay you. But just as serious, if not more so, once the time limit on payment is up the Order is printed in the *London Gazette*, and circulated to all banks and other financial institutions. As you can imagine, being 'Gazetted', as it's called, does little for your credit rating!

If we had received the notice of the Winding Up Order, we would obviously have paid the £90 within the time limit. Yes, I would have found it extremely galling to pay for faulty goods, but the time and money involved in fighting it would have amounted to far more than £90, and sometimes standing up for a principle is just not worth it. But the Winding Up Order wasn't sent to Pineapple. It was sent to our registered office, which happened to be the address of a firm that we were only using on an occasional consultancy basis. So if any mail arrived there for us, they assumed it couldn't be urgent, and kept it until there was enough to be worth sending on.

By the time the Winding Up Order reached us, the time limit was up and the whole procedure was underway. Luckily, all our suppliers had enough confidence in us not to turn up at the hearing (where, in fact, the order was thrown out on a technicality; they'd got the name of the company wrong) and demand their money. But at the time when Pineapple's share price was falling, the fact that we had been 'Gazetted' was the final straw in our dealings with our bank and they withdrew our working facility.

As a direct result of that experience, we moved our registered office to our own premises. Most small businesses use their accountants' address as their registered office, but you don't need to and at least if you use your own business address, there's no chance of important mail failing to reach you.

When it comes to embarking upon litigation yourself, my advice generally would be to try to avoid it if possible. It is time- and energy-consuming and expensive. No matter how right you are, and even if you win, it will cost you. On the other hand, you must always take action against anyone using your name or trying to imitate you. We have sued a few times – one manufacturer who was producing 'Silver Pineapple' tracksuits and various people who opened 'Pineapple Dance Centres'. It's costly, but vital for the future of your business.

Anita Roddick feels very strongly about this sort of confusion. Having taken as her creed from the very beginning 'Never dilute your image', she wasn't prepared to let imitators do it for her, and took immediate action against anyone trying to trade on the Body Shop name, or logo.

People

Whether you're running a hairdressing salon, or a multi-million pound hi-tech export company, the most important thing to remember is that people are your business. Ultimately it's people that create your profits and your staff can make or break you. 'Personnel' isn't a factor you start thinking about later, once your business is beginning to grow. It's something you must think about very carefully before you even take on your first employee. After all the person who answers your 'phone, or deals with your customers face to face *is* your business as far as the customers are concerned and they will judge you by his or her performance. If that employee is on the ball, friendly and efficient, he or she will create a good impression. If the person is bored, rude or sloppy, then that's how your customers will view your business.

Finding the people you need

You've reached the stage where your business is beginning to grow and you can no longer cope on your own. You need an assistant, but before you employ anyone, it is well worth taking the time not only to think about the sort of person you need, but also what you want them to do.

In a new business that's growing, it's almost impossible to have 'one person/one job', but even so, it's very important when you take people on that you have a clear idea of what they're going to do. What you don't want are two or three people, all doing bits of everything and tripping over each other in the process.

Building the workforce is a costly business so don't employ too many too soon. You need to have a very clear idea of what your staff is going to cost you. Look at job ads in the paper, ask around, and get a good idea of the going rate. Also remember that National Insurance contributions will add 10%.

Finding the right people is the key to a successful business.

In my experience I have found it better to rely on contacts when you are looking for people, than to go through agencies or to advertise. Also some of my best people have either walked through the door or just written in.

As your career develops, you need to build up your area of expertise, specialize, and delegate. But at the beginning, it's important not to be too proud to muck in. I booked the studios, took the memberships, sold the dancewear and orange juice, cleaned the loos – and did the books at home in the evening!

My first assistant was the sister of a friend and she

and I were the total workforce when Pineapple first opened.

EMPLOYMENT AGENCIES

The first place you might think of looking are employment agencies. Some are extremely good, and take the trouble to send you people who actually meet the criteria you have laid down. Others are not quite so good and seem to simply send you the first half dozen people who walk through their office door that day, none of whom is remotely suitable. On occasion I have recruited suitable people through employment agencies, but generally speaking, I have never found them to be particularly helpful.

After my first PA was poached by a competitor I took on an ex-dancer called Amanda who was wonderful, but when she left to have a baby I did try an agency. They sent me several girls and none of them was right. One girl on their books who was disappointed the agency had not sent her for an interview wrote to me direct, even though the agency had assured her I had seen her CV (which I hadn't) and told her that I wasn't interested. I was impressed by this initiative and saw her. She was just right. This was Yve Elliott who was an excellent PA and is now running Pineapple's PR and Promotion department. Of course the agency still wanted to charge me a huge fee!

Agencies are expensive – they'll charge you between 15% and 17.5% of the first year's salary, and although most of the reputable agencies will refund part of the money if that person leaves within three months, it can be a costly way of recruiting staff.

JOB CENTRES AND YTS

There are, of course, job centres, but I've never employed anyone that way and other businesswomen I know have had very little success. If you are starting up a business and money is very tight, it's worth thinking about the YTS scheme. A sixteen or seventeen year old comes to work for you for two years or one year respectively, and is paid between £27.30 and £35 by the Department of Employment. In return, you are expected to offer on-the-job training, and in the case of the two-year scheme, allow the trainee time off to attend college or a skill centre during the second year. You have to satisfy the Manpower Services Commission that you can provide the standard of training they are looking for before they will give you a trainee, and they will pay you about £250 a year into the bargain.

People's experiences of YTS trainees vary widely – some employers find them more trouble than they're worth, but others find them invaluable. The fact that they come straight from school with no work experience means that you can train them in your own way of doing things – you don't have to spend time getting them to unlearn bad habits. There's no doubt that some employers do view the scheme as a source of cheap labour and, when the year or two years is up, simply replace the old trainee with a new one. Others make a point of not accepting a trainee unless there is at least the chance of a permanent job at the end of it – assuming, of course, the trainee proves good enough to fill it.

SITS. VAC.

Advertising for staff in specialist magazines – *Accountancy Age* or *Drapers' Record*, for instance – or newspapers like *The Times*, the *Guardian* or the London *Evening*

Standard which feature job ads for particular professions on different days, will probably be beyond your means when you're starting out, but a small ad in the local newspaper is an inexpensive way of recruiting staff.

Judi Jurak, who runs the computer services consultancy Syslib Ltd in Leeds, placed a job ad in her local paper, and gave no phone number. 'We then interviewed the people who'd had the initiative to get our number from directory enquiries and ring up.'

I personally like people to write in because I believe that what they write *and* their handwriting are both important clues to their character. But speaking on the telephone can tell you a lot about a person too.

Lois Jacobs, Managing Director of Hamilton Perry Conferences, doesn't usually follow up letters asking for jobs that aren't addressed to her personally. 'If they haven't taken the trouble to find out my name, then they almost certainly haven't got the initiative we want.'

But I still find that word of mouth is probably the most effective way of finding staff. Christina Smith finds that most of her senior staff come through personal recommendation from friends or acquaintances:

'Some people say it's an unprofessional, haphazard way of recruiting people, but as far as I can see from my long years of experience, the only difference between my way and getting them through an agency is that if it doesn't work out, my way hasn't cost me anything!'

I'm also a great believer in talent spotting, and making a note of good people you come across in any situation. I remember having lunch with a friend who runs a very successful business. He was impressed with the waitress who served us and when we were leaving, gave her his card and said 'If you're ever looking for a job, give me a ring.' (Well, I assume that's what he meant!)

As to whether it's a good idea to employ family or friends, opinions vary. My inclination is to say it's not a good idea – if it doesn't work out, how do you fire your sister or your best friend's husband? Ann Levick, Managing Director of Panmed Ltd, agrees. 'I've employed people I know in the past, but I will never ever do it again. For one thing you put more faith in them than you would in strangers, so if it isn't working out, it takes you longer to do anything about it. In a number of cases, I left it until I was at the end of my tether and that meant that when the crunch came, I didn't deal with it calmly and objectively. It also meant it was impossible to keep the friendship.'

But other people disagree. Anita Roddick says that, given the hectic life she leads, the only way she can be sure of seeing her family and friends is to have them working in the company! But then her background is Italian and she grew up working alongside her brothers and sisters in her mama's café, so it seems perfectly natural to her.

CV or not CV

At the risk of depressing anyone who has spent whole evenings polishing their *curriculum vitae* I don't actually lay a great deal of store by them. My schooling was interrupted by a severe bout of whooping cough when I was fourteen. I missed three months' schooling at a critical time and it was difficult to catch up. So I felt I had to move on and, at fifteen, went to commercial college. Fortunately my parents were very supportive and didn't pressure me or make me feel I was a disappointment.

I have always found that however bad you are feeling about one door closing for you, another will always open if you are determined enough. And I am not the only person heading up a major organization without many or indeed any 'O' levels. (I'm in good company with Richard Branson and Sir Terence Conran to name but two!)

I am not interested in where people went to school or how many GCE's they've got, and that's just as well really. One young man I know failed all his 'O' levels, but on his CV he listed all those he had taken! No-one bothered to check in his case, and I'm sure 99 employers out of 100 never bother to ask for 'O' or 'A' level certificates. Obviously if you're employing an accountant, for example, professional qualifications are important, but other than that, I find them irrelevant and even potentially misleading.

But a CV can give you important clues if you read between the lines. I would be very wary, for example, of someone who'd had lots of jobs because it suggests that either they've been fired rather too often or they've got no staying power. Certainly it suggests that loyalty isn't one of their strong suits, and loyalty is something I value highly. Some people applying for jobs know that employers are sometimes a bit suspicious of someone who's had a string of jobs and so leave a few out, but careful questioning and checking of dates when you take up references can usually unearth those.

I'm not keen on employing people with hobbies. While I think people have to work hard and play hard, I am inclined to think that real hobbies are for retired people! There just isn't enough time to have a career and hobbies too. If someone wants to go off parachute-jumping or pot-holing every weekend, it does suggest to me that they aren't ready to give a job the kind of commitment I'm looking for. And it also suggests that they might be in late on a Monday morning more often than I'd like.

If you're looking for someone to do a practical job, then once you've selected those you want to see, it's relatively easy because you ask for a specimen of their work. When I was thinking of hiring someone to run the café at Covent Garden, for example, I asked her to cook various things and make a salad. That was fine. What I didn't know until she started work was that she chain-smoked as she cooked!

When I wanted a pattern cutter, I asked the applicants to cut some patterns and looked at the finished garments. In those cases, never mind the personality, what comes first is the practical skill.

With other jobs, though, like a PA, receptionist, shop manageress, or any management job, personality does matter and the only answer is . . .

The dreaded interview

There have been millions of words written about the interview as psychological warfare – making the interviewee's chair much lower than your own so that they are forced to look up at you, making them sit with the sun in their eyes so you can see them but they can't see you, placing their chair so they can't actually sit on it without moving it in one direction or another – but I suspect these methods are probably more revealing about the interviewer than the interviewee. I often end up interviewing people in the most chaotic conditions but I do find the way they handle this is a good indication of how they will cope later on.

FIRST IMPRESSIONS

While we all know that we shouldn't judge books by their covers, there is no doubt that the first impression someone makes on you when he or she walks through your door is very important.

Can you believe that this woman is the very neat, orderly worker she says she is when she has ladders in her tights and her hair needs washing? It is important that people look as if they've taken trouble with their appearance, even if it is rather bizarre. For certain jobs, a magenta mohican hairstyle would be all right as long as it was well done. People who take trouble with their appearance are more likely to take trouble with their work, though we're all too familiar with the secretary or receptionist who sees her work as an irritating interruption to filing her nails or doing her make-up.

BODY LANGUAGE

'Body Language' is something you should be aware of throughout your career, as it is vital for developing successful working relationships, as well as assessing business contacts or job applicants yourself.

Remember always to be attentive – if you look bored during an important business meeting you are hardly likely to clinch the deal or to impress the bank manager!

I always find body language a very important indicator of personality and attitude. Someone who creeps into the room timidly as though they don't think they ought to be there is unlikely to be outgoing and have bags of initiative. Equally, someone who swans into the office as though she owns the place and plonks her elbows on the desk is also unlikely to get the job.

One man came to see me for a management position in the company. He walked in with his tie loose and his top shirt button undone, and then sat with one arm over the back of the chair, just exuding arrogance. You know you'll have problems with anyone who sits like that. Needless to say he didn't get the job!

Anita Roddick has a problem with people who are slower of thought and speech than she is, which is probably about 95% of us!

'But I do try to stop myself racing on, and give people more time.'

NOW TELL ME ABOUT YOURSELF

There are probably as many styles of interviewing as there are interviewers, and I think you only arrive at the one that suits you by trial and error. I like to get people chatting about themselves – about why they're changing jobs, where they live, travelling times, their personal lives, and if they've got children, what arrangements they have for looking after them. If a woman has a family and needs to travel a long distance then inevitably I would be keen to ensure that she has established the appropriate support systems that would allow her to be as flexible in her work as someone who's single and lives down the road. If you are running a small business, you simply cannot afford to carry people, and women with children who have not organized their domestic commitments are potentially less reliable than single women or men. Of course it's unfair that child care facilities are so appalling, and that women have to carry the burden, but, unfortunately, that is the stark reality at the moment although things are improving.

It's always difficult to tell everything from an interview, as people are often nervous and act out of character. However, I always make a point of asking them if they have visited any of the Pineapples – as you would expect them to have at least done a little background research into the company, and it shows if they have used their common sense and initiative!

I also ask about health because I'm not very tolerant of people who are always off sick. I am quite honest about it, and if people know they do take quite a bit of time off, they'll realize themselves that they're not right for the job.

It's important to listen carefully to what people say. When they are telling you about their previous jobs, do they run down their former bosses and companies? Were things that went wrong always someone else's fault, or do they always emerge on top? Either they are paragons, in which case why are they looking for a job, or else they have a problem which you can well do without.

Sidney Burstein who runs Browns fashion stores with his wife Joan, says when he interviews people he looks for 3 A's – Aware, Alert, Alive. I look for 3 C's and an E – Commitment, Communication, Common-sense and Energy.

If I'm honest, I depend to a large extent on instinct. When I was looking for a sales manager, I interviewed two people. I liked one of them very much – he felt right. But when I told a fellow director about him he said, 'Never employ a sales manager who's been out of work for five months because if he was any good he'd have been snapped up months ago.' I said, 'Maybe he's been waiting for the right job to come along' and I was right. He had been waiting for something to inspire him. I took him on and he was absolutely terrific!

GRAPHOLOGY

I like to get my instincts confirmed if possible, and as I've said before I am a great believer in looking at handwriting. Indeed, I'm not alone – companies such as Warburg Bank, Royal Mail and Heron Corporation now get people's handwriting analysed before they appoint them to management positions. I always get people to write something down for me, even if it's only their name and address. I now know the basics of graphology but even before I did I felt handwriting was an import-ant clue – if it was all over the place, then I felt the person probably was too, and so wouldn't be right for me. If the handwriting slopes backwards, the person is likely to be rather plodding without a great deal of get up and go, but of course for some jobs these qualities are ideal.

ASTROLOGY

If it's an important job, and I'm not one hundred per cent sure about who to appoint, then I might ask Claire, the Pineapple psychic consultant, to do an astrological chart.

In the past, I have given her the person's birthdate after I've made the decision. But then, a year or so ago, I gave her the birthdate of someone I had just taken on and Claire told me that, although she was perfectly capable of doing the job, she would cause tremendous problems in the company as a result of her personal life. Just a couple of weeks later, she and another member of the management team (who was already married) fell madly in love and the complications that ensued meant that neither of them had any time for Pineapple and obviously they both had to leave! Since then I usually try to involve Claire before I commit myself.

After the revelations about Nancy Reagan's astrologer in 1988, I feel I'm in good company, though I know colleagues with 'formal' business backgrounds still think my methods are ludicrous. But I have to say I am as successful as they are in my choice of staff.

A friend of mine who has a large company was looking for a sales manager, which was a key position, and he did everything by the book – interviewed the man three or four times, took him and his wife out to dinner and so on. He took the man on, only to find that he moped and whinged, had always got a headache and couldn't put a letter together to save his life. (His wife had written the job application.) He has lost confidence to such an extent that he can't face going through all that again, so he is doing the sales manager's job himself.

THE INTERVIEWEE

There is an old joke about an actor who goes to an audition and is offered the job. 'Oh no,' he says, shocked, 'I don't do parts. I only do auditions.' There are some people who interview so outstandingly well that you don't realize until it's too late that they can't actually do the job.

Judi Jurak of Syslib is always wary when she finds herself thinking 'Yes, this is the one' early on in an interview.

Christina Smith finds herself following the same pattern again and again:

'When they walk in I almost always think, "Oh, this person won't do at all!" And then half an hour later, I find myself liking them, no matter what they're like or how unsuitable they are. I can only really start to think about them seriously and form a judgment when they're not there.'

According to Anita Roddick, so many people are brilliant at selling themselves to such an extent that 'you don't know who you've got into bed with for three or four months after they start!' Her defence against it is to disarm them:

'First of all they are thrown by the way I'm dressed – jeans, sweatshirt, whatever – and that is quite deliberate because you also have to give them some clues as to the kind of company it is. And then the latest thing we're using is the Marcel Proust questionnaire, a list of about twenty seemingly daft questions, such as "How would you like to die?", "What is your favourite flower?" and "Who is your heroine from fiction?". They've come expecting to give you their carefully prepared sales pitch, and they find they're having to answer off the top of their heads. And it is quite revealing. If they try to be smart-arsed and say "My hero is Adolf Eichmann, or Biggles", we know we would have problems.

'We are different; we want people who are loving, people who have a commitment to the environment, to education, to the community – for heaven's sake we even have departments with those names – so people who are embarrassed even to talk about such things are not for us. We can't live with people who are acerbic, and we are very uncomfortable with cynics.

'A lot of it is instinct. I don't give a toss if they don't know anything about anything. If they are open and have a child-like curiosity about things – not that tired old feeling of "I've done it all before . . ." – then they'll be easy to work with. Energy is what I look for, and passion.'

THE SALES PITCH

It's very easy to get so wrapped up in trying to decide whether or not you want the person in front of you to work for your company that you forget that they may not necessarily want to work for you. They will probably have other interviews lined up, so, in case you do decide this is the person you want, you have to sell the job and your company as well. That's not as straightforward as it sounds, though, because I also believe it's best to point out the down side of the job right from the start. From the earliest days of Pineapple, I've always told potential employees, 'It's really hard work: twenty-four hours a day, seven days a week. It's not at all glamorous, there's no social life.' If you paint too rosy a picture, then the person you employ is unlikely to stay once they discover the reality and so you'll be forced to go through the whole, time-consuming, expensive, tedious process all over again. The art is in striking exactly the right balance between pointing out the drawbacks and selling the pluses.

Unless it's your first employee, perhaps the most important question to ask yourself, after 'Can this person do the job?' is 'Will she fit in with the people already working here?' If yours is a fairly free-flowing organization where everyone mucks in, you probably don't want someone whose whole working life has been spent in very rigidly-structured, hierarchical companies.

Once your company is big enough to have department heads, then you must allow them to hire and fire their own junior staff. It's difficult even to recommend someone to them, because they might think you're trying to put a spy in their particular camp, and rather than improving the person's chances of getting the job, you might make them a lot worse.

EENY MEENY MINEY MO

Once the interviews are over, you have to make up your mind, and that's the tricky bit. You might hope that one candidate stands head and shoulders above the rest and therefore the decision virtually makes itself. But there is a problem. Just because she is the best of the bunch doesn't mean that she is right for the job. In fact, it is probably better if you wind up with two very strong candidates and have to choose between them. They throw light on each other's strengths and weaknesses and in the process help you to clarify exactly what you want the person to do and how he or she would fit in.

For a junior job, obviously, there's no point in agonizing endlessly – the best thing to do is take the person on a trial basis and see how it goes, though obviously that's much easier to do if he or she is not currently working and doesn't have to leave a job to come to you. With a senior job, it is worth taking the time to get it right. If only one candidate emerges, then put her on hold and try again. There's a chance that in the meantime she might take another job of course, but on balance it's probably better to lose someone potentially good than to take on someone who is actually useless. I've been pressured to make decisions about hiring people that agencies have found when I knew they weren't right. I was told, 'The agencies are the experts, they know these people and besides there isn't time to carry on looking.'

But it takes a lot more time to undo the mess that results from taking on the wrong person! Don't be rushed into employing someone just because you're desperate. If you're not sure, see some more people. A man rang me recently for a reference for someone I had fired for dishonesty. I told the caller exactly why I had fired him and he said 'Are you sure you can't recommend *anything* about him? I'm really desperate . . .' I said 'No-one is *that* desperate.'

In a sense, choosing an employee is a bit like choosing a husband or a wife. Don't take people on thinking that you'll be able to change the bits you don't like, because you won't. The best you can hope for is that you can build on their strengths and prevent their weaknesses from getting any worse.

Reference points

Always, always, always take up references. I fired one woman on the spot because she had her hand in the till (she took me to an industrial tribunal because of it, but she lost) and to my astonishment she gave me as a referee, obviously thinking that the company she'd applied to wouldn't follow it up. Anyway, they did ring me and I told them what my experience of her had been. But I do know since then that someone has given her a job.

Don't accept references that are handed to you at the interview – it's too easy for people to take a piece of headed notepaper from places where they've worked and write their own. If you do take up references and get them in writing, study them closely. Employers are reluctant to write openly damning references, because they could find themselves being sued for defamation by the former employee in question. In one case in 1987 an ex-employee sued his former bosses over a reference which he claimed had kept him out of work for two years. He lost, but the company had all the expense and aggravation of fighting the case. A former employer may be willing, though, to damn by faint praise: 'quite a good worker', 'seems honest' or 'carried out the tasks she was requested to do'.

Look, too, for the ambiguous phrase. 'Responds well to instructions' can also be read as 'shows no initiative'.

'The company that gets Mary Smith to work for it will be very lucky indeed!' can certainly be read two ways. You should also look carefully for what they *don't* say. If you're looking for a production manager, for example, and the reference goes on at length about his production capabilities, but says nothing about his management skills, beware. In general terms, if a reference doesn't mention punctuality, good nature, or most crucially, honesty, there is almost certainly a reason why.

Since you are running your own business, and don't have to justify any mistakes to anyone, an off-the-record telephone reference is much more valuable than a written one. People are much more likely to be open with you on the phone, because, although technically they could still be sued for slander if they give a bad reference, producing the evidence is much more difficult. Even so, some employers, out of the kindness of their hearts, are still reluctant to give anyone a bad reference unless they were really dreadful, but they will reply honestly to direct questions, so you need to know what to ask. A good opening question is 'I'm thinking of employing Mary Smith as a shop manageress. What do you think?' Ask the former employer if he'd mind telling you why she left, and, most important, whether or not he would employ her again.

If he says he would employ her again like a shot, she is obviously a good worker, but you need to add 'and in the same job?' Maybe he would employ her again as a sales assistant but not as a manageress because while she was good with customers, she was hopeless at stock control.

Sometimes it's pointless ringing former employers and asking for a reference. If they're upset and angry that the person wants to leave, for example, they may give them a bad reference out of spite. Our pattern cutter and machinist came from the same company, and I know their boss was furious because he rang up and accused us of stealing his girls, so obviously there wasn't much point in asking him for a reference.

Putting them on probation

In most cases, taking people on for a trial period is a good idea. All the shop assistants come on a month's trial, and in the past I have taken some senior staff on three months' trial. I think within three months you know one way or the other. A probationary period can be helpful for both sides. It makes you aware that it is an induction period, and that you have a responsibility to the new employee to show her how the company works, what the do's and don'ts are, who she is reporting to and exactly what is expected of her. It's really unfair and inefficient simply to say 'Just pick it up as you go along.' From your point of view, the fact that she knows she is on trial is likely to make her more willing to listen, to do things the way you want them done and to adapt to the company.

At the end of the trial period, assuming that you want to keep her on, it's worth taking the time to appraise her work so far, and tell her how she is doing. There are a number of books on management *'One Minute Manager'* by Kenneth Blanchard and Spencer Johnson (published by Fontana) is one – the basic message of which boils down to: 'accentuate the positive' – give praise for what an employee is doing well, and then deal with the areas where there is room for improvement. That way you can stop bad habits before they become too deeply ingrained.

Finding . . . keeping . . .

Given how difficult, time-consuming and expensive it is to find good staff, it obviously makes sense to try very hard to keep them. First of all, you have to understand that it's not their own business and naturally they will not be as committed as you are. So you have to find ways of motivating them.

All the surveys on what keeps staff motivated point to the same conclusion – people who feel they are valued, who feel they have a degree of control over their working lives and their future, people who feel they are treated as people and not as machines, work harder than people who don't.

Anita Roddick sums up her style of management as 'love, humour, energy and passion':

'"Love" should be shouted down the corridors of big corporations. Business has got to humanize itself. We work on the "feminine principles" by, to quote Ralph Waldo Emerson, "putting our love where our labour is", by being intuitive and ignoring the aggressiveness of today's business philosophy.'

INCENTIVES

How do you make your employees feel valued? One very obvious answer is money. If you can pay them more than the going local rate for the job then it's easy.

But if you've just started out in business, and money is tight, then you can't afford to do that.

It can be very difficult. If you've got good people who work very hard, they are worth more to you than you can afford to pay them, even if they are earning the same, if not more, than they'd get elsewhere. If you can give them a big pay rise one year, then it's only human nature that they'll expect at least the same the next year, and if you can't afford to give them as much they're disappointed.

More and more, we are building incentive schemes into the pay structure. As a public company we were able to offer people share options, so they had a stake in the company. The harder they worked, the better the company did and the more they benefited. Now that I have privatized, I have set up a bonus scheme for the studio receptionists and the staff in the shops. It's working very well. If the shop is getting low on a fast-selling item, the girls are quick to tell me about it because they know if they run out, they're unlikely to meet their target for the week and therefore won't get their bonus.

There are various schemes you can adopt that relate reward to performance. One Body Shop franchisee in Canada, for example, set up an average sales scheme. If the average sale in the shop went up from $5 one day to $6 the next, the staff would get a bonus point. If by the end of the month they had twenty points, every member of staff got a cash bonus. It's a very good scheme because it's a group effort, the staff all encourage each other; and from an employer's point of view it makes sound business sense. If you pay your six employees £20 each, it would cost you £120 – a small fraction of the increase in takings that result from the higher average sale!

SELF-ESTEEM

It is worth remembering that for some people, money is symbolic, too. One woman who worked for us asked for a large rise that we couldn't afford to pay. When I told her so, she said, 'Don't you think I'm worth that much?' I said, 'It's not that – I think you're terrific, you really earn your money and you're worth much more. But if we're being commercial as we have to be, this is as much as we can afford to pay you right now, and as much as you'd get anywhere else for doing the same job. In a few years, when we're making more money, there'll be all sorts of opportunities for bonuses and so on.'

She was quite happy then. What she wanted was recognition of her worth as a person, a boost to her self-esteem.

SHOWING YOU CARE

I remember seeing a television programme a few years ago about what motivated people at work and I was very surprised to see that money wasn't at the top of the list. The most important thing was what they called 'hygiene', which covered working conditions, environment and so on. There is a famous example in the book *In Search of Excellence* (by Thomas Peters and Robert Waterman, published by Harper and Row), where the management turned up the lights in the factory because they thought it would be better for the employees, and productivity went up. After some discussion about whether the lighting level was better or not, they turned it down again, and productivity went up again. It had nothing to do with lighting, and everything to do with the fact that the workforce felt management cared about them and their environment.

If your company is small enough, of course you should know all your employees by name and you should know a bit about them – whether they're married, if they have children and so on. You should also know if someone's personal problems are affecting their work. Recently, one of our staff who had always been a marvellous worker seemed to be on another planet, and her work had deteriorated to such a point that I even wondered about letting her go. Finally I called her in and asked what the matter was. It turned out that she was pregnant and had been frightened to tell me. Once I'd told her that her job was safe, she was back to her old self right away. She had been so scared of losing her job that she had almost lost it anyway!

Mind you, I don't always believe that to understand all is to forgive all. If your warehouseman keeps taking days off because his marriage is breaking up, you can sympathize with his predicament, but on the other hand if your business is grinding to a halt because he isn't there, you have to consider the rest of the staff's future, not to mention your own.

Sheelah Wilson who ran the Manchester model agency for which I started working at fifteen drummed it into us – 'Don't take your personal problems to work, because an employer doesn't want to know. If you're upset over a row with your boyfriend last night, keep it to yourself. If your mother died yesterday, either go to work and look cheerful or don't go.'

As an employer you have to do your bit, but you

really don't have the time to get closely involved in their problems.

This is Anita Roddick's view:

'People aren't an asset – they *are* the company and what hurts them hurts us. One of my assistants knows exactly what's going on and keeps me informed. As long as you keep your units small, you can do that. We are very sociable as a company. We have darts teams and football clubs, and we do community projects together. As Noel Coward said, "Work is more fun than fun," so it ends up spreading into every area of your life!'

Sophie Mirman of the Sock Shop believes that you keep your staff motivated by being so yourself:

'I think that really does filter right through a company. We are tremendously enthusiastic and there is great enthusiasm in the company. Everyone is pulling in the same direction – there's no bitchiness because no-one has anything to prove. We take on very good people who are confident and secure in their own abilities.

'We also do things like running a Mastermind competition. Last Christmas there were regional heats and a grand final in London, with a first prize of an all-expenses-paid weekend in New York for two. The specialist subject was the Sock Shop and I must say the contestants were terrific. I was still thinking about question one while they were on question five!'

She also believes that one essential ingredient in keeping staff motivated is good communication – making sure everyone knows what's happening in the company, and also making sure that people feel their opinions are listened to and taken seriously:

'All our managers come to head office once every six weeks for a meeting with us and the management team here. We talk about what's happening on our side of the business, and they tell us what's happening on theirs – what merchandise is going well, what isn't, what sort of things they'd like more of, and so on.'

Anita Roddick has made communication into an art form:

'Communication is the key to our company. We have our own video and film company, and a video cassette called "Talking Shop", in which we tell all the staff what's happening, is sent to all the three hundred shops worldwide every month. We also have a bi-monthly talk sheet in which the staff tell us and their colleagues what's happening from their perspective – we hear the complaints, the challenges and ideas for improvement. Much of it is critical, which is great – the anarchists are the great change-makers! They annoy and irritate until something is done! We also have news flashes that go out all the time, and tours of the shops – management by walking about, I call it. My backside doesn't see my office chair for days at a time!'

You may think it's too obvious to mention but praise is terribly important in making people feel valued. You may think that you employ people to do the job properly, and so why should you praise them when they do? The answer is that it costs nothing and really does keep people motivated. Christina Smith believes it's terribly important and admits that she isn't as liberal with it as she ought to be:

'In fact I tend to praise people I think less of than I praise those I think well of, I suppose because I expect the latter to do well.'

Promotion from within

One reason staff leave is that they are bored with their jobs and, if they're ambitious, believe that they'll have to move to get on. This is often a problem with PAs – a good one won't be content to stay a PA for ever. In the past I've solved this by giving them another project to work on as well. Yve Elliott, who was my PA for five years, started helping with the fashion PR and now she looks after that exclusively.

The problem was of course that I was without a PA – who are as most people in business would agree the most difficult people to find. After a few people didn't work out, I realized the perfect PA, Shirlee Deacon, had been here for some years working in the Accounts Department!

My first manager at Covent Garden studios, David Paton, had worked his way up part-timing as a dish-washer during rest periods from his career as a dancer. It wasn't long before Pineapple was the obvious place for people to call if they wanted dancers for shows, TV and videos, etc., and again by sheer demand The Pineapple Agency began. David was eager to run it and has made a great success of it. David's girlfriend Becky Willis (now his wife) was helping in the office having given up her career with the Royal Ballet. She stepped into David's job running the Covent Garden studios and she now looks after the teachers and bookings for all the Pineapple Centres.

Good people are too precious to lose, so if you find someone is getting frustrated and beginning to look elsewhere, talk to them, find out what they want to do and see if there isn't something else within the company for them. Christina Smith is a great believer in promoting from within.

'It's cheaper apart from anything else – recruiting and training new people is such an expensive and time-consuming business. If your business is as varied as ours is, you can expose people to different facets. Sometimes it's purely a question of personalities – they don't get on with their manager – so it's very easy to move them into another shop. I get very angry if I find people have left for that reason. In fact now I insist on seeing all the termination notices (we have them on both sides) so that I can spot it in time and if possible prevent it happening.'

We lost a very good sales assistant from one of the shops because the manager was treating her badly and then a couple of weeks later we had to fire him because it turned out he simply hadn't been doing his job. So we lost a good person unnecessarily.

HOW CAN YOU DO THIS TO ME?

You have to accept that sometimes good staff will leave in spite of all your efforts. It's important then not to take it personally. In the early days, one of our top salesgirls was head-hunted and I was really upset. But I've learnt to be more philosophical about it. One key person – Danka – who had been with us almost from the start, left a year ago – she was offered an opportunity she simply couldn't turn down. I was upset, but then I thought, 'It's the right move for her now, she'll always be a friend, and she's given us ten marvellous years.' (Incidentally, she has now returned to work at Pineapple full time!)

Although obviously you care passionately about what you do, you must accept that you and your business are two separate things. Eighteen years of modelling was very good training for that. If you didn't get a job it was because they wanted someone taller/thinner/fatter/older/blonde. It wasn't because there was anything wrong with you. You were disappointed, obviously, but you didn't take it personally.

THE PETER PRINCIPLE (PROMOTION)

In your efforts to hang on to good people, you have to beware of the Peter Principle described by top American businessman Laurence J. Peter in the Sixties, which means, basically, promoting people beyond their capability. Someone who is a brilliant salesman may not have any managerial skills, so if you promote him to sales manager, you'll not only have lost your best salesman, you'll have acquired a lousy sales manager too.

Anyone who is ambitious relishes a challenge and on the administrative side that usually means taking on more responsibility. From my side of the desk that's called delegation.

Delegation not abdication

You hear it said many times that the key to successful management is the art of delegation. A lot of people think it's simply a question of getting someone else to do something for you. It isn't. The art is in giving responsibility for particular areas of work once you have mastered them yourself, to someone whom you have trained and who is now as good at it as you are, if not better. It's a very serious business and you musn't let go of the rope until you are sure she really knows what she's doing. Then you let go, give her plenty of rope but with regular feedback and find that she's doing it better than you ever did. In other words delegate – but don't abdicate responsibility.

At the end of the day you're the boss and you are 100% responsible if things go wrong. You can't blame others if you've just left them to it and have not given the proper training.

IN SEARCH OF EXCELLENCE

I know that some people in business are afraid to employ people who might be better than they are at certain things because they would feel threatened, but I really can't understand that attitude. I know Pineapple's success depends on the quality of the people who work here, so I want the very best I can get. It's my dream to find people who have better ideas, better ways of doing things that actually add to the business.

Sophie Mirman couldn't agree more:

'Last year, the only sock colour I selected personally for the autumn range turned out to be the slowest selling colour of all! And I'm delighted because it means that I now have a team of people who are much better in the area of design than I am. It has been a very definite policy always to take on people in each area of the business who are better at it than either Richard or I.'

COMMUNICATION

We have a saying here: 'Assumption is the mother of all f---ups!' 'Oh, I assumed it would be all right . . .' 'I assumed you were taking care of that . . .' The message must be – communicate!

There is a lot of truth in the well-known story about four people named everybody, somebody, anybody and nobody. There was an important job to be done and everybody was asked to do it. Everybody was sure somebody would do it. Anybody could have done it but nobody did it. Somebody got angry about that because it was everybody's job. Everybody thought anybody could do it, but nobody realized that everybody wouldn't do it. It ended up that everybody blamed somebody when nobody did what anybody could have done!

Weekly management meetings are vital and must be minuted with initials in the action column as to who is responsible for what. You have to get the message across to people that if they're not sure, they must always check with you first. And even if they are sure, and it involves spending money, they must check with you anyway. You must always be accessible. It's dangerous if people think they shouldn't bother you. I say to people 'Please bother me!' It's a very difficult balance to strike – knowing when to give people more rope and when to rein them in a bit – but it is crucial to the success of your business.

When we did our first catalogue I asked one of my managers to organize it, sketch out a design, get some costings and so on. So, eventually, he showed me a sketched layout. I said, 'Well, the real thing will probably look better . . .' and he said, 'No, this is it.' He'd already given the go-ahead to the printers and committed us to several thousand pounds. What should have happened is that he should have used his initiative in getting the whole thing organized and costed, and then shown it to me for final approval *before* he spent the money.

Christina Smith is also a great believer in monitoring things as they go along:

'Some of my senior colleagues complain that I interfere too much, but it seems to me only common sense to check how things are going. On a very simple level, if you ask someone to do some artwork, and when you check on how they're getting on, you find they're doing it in purple when you asked for red, you can point that out. Otherwise they may spend three days doing it before you know it's wrong. I'm a great believer in nipping problems in the bud.'

But if you are going to encourage people to use their initiative, you must accept that there will be some mistakes. All you can do is set up systems of checks and balances that will prevent them from being too costly. If you stifle all initiative, then neither your staff nor your company will grow. Fear of failure is a very powerful and negative force, so you should be prepared to praise genuine initiative even if it fails, otherwise you undermine and de-motivate people.

You will always have people who create problems, but you have to weigh that up against their talent and contribution. If the pluses outweigh the minuses, learn to live with it.

NO HIDING PLACE

Making mistakes is one thing. Not doing the job properly is something else. If someone is skiving in a small company, it's just not fair on everyone else. I have no patience with people who shirk, or want to read their book, or extend their lunch hour bit by bit. I have said to people, 'You want to go and work for a large company where you can hide and no-one will notice. We are a small company and there's too much at stake for all of us to carry passengers.'

But before you act, you must be really sure of your facts, know exactly what's been going on, and don't just go on a whim or a feeling. It's something that no-one enjoys doing, but you must act quickly, and not let it fester. You can't be in a mood with the person, or avoid her because you know you've got to sit down with her and talk about the problem. That's just not professional. You need to be sure that the job description was clear – even if the job is to do a variety of things and muck in whenever the need arises – and that she did know what was expected of her. And then you need to find out what the problem is, and let her state her case. Maybe there has been a misunderstanding or she will admit she can't cope with the job and then you can take appropriate action.

NO SECOND CHANCE

I must say I am not a believer in second chances. I have never seen an instance where someone has been given a second chance and it has worked. I remember we had a shop assistant who was always late and then, when she did finally come in, sat reading a book. When the manager decided to fire her, she burst into tears, and begged for another chance, so he gave in. She continued to be late and continued to read her book! The manager couldn't believe how she had let him down and certainly never gave anyone else a second chance.

THE BIG 'E'

Before you fire someone you must check your legal position. If you have under twenty employees you may sack staff any time in the first two years without notice. Over twenty – you may sack staff any time within the first year. After one year you have to issue formal warnings in writing first, otherwise they can bring a case for unfair dismissal against you at an Industrial Tribunal. The Department of Employment publishes a number of very helpful free booklets on employment law which are well worth getting hold of.

No-one enjoys firing people. It is one of the most unpleasant aspects of being a boss. Anita Roddick absolutely loathes it:

'Once you've decided, you don't sleep for two days, but you take the responsibility to do it yourself. And you go straight in, you don't put it off till after lunch. I still find it as daunting as ever because if someone was a really awful person, they wouldn't be there in the first place. But I do learn from it – if nothing else, I learn what I *don't* want – for example, I would *never ever* take on anyone trained in a large retail multiple again because they are so controlled and protected by a system that stops them from being accountable and from thinking on their feet!'

Sophie Mirman feels the same way about firing staff:
'Nobody likes firing people, but some people don't mind it whereas I really hate it. That's why we are so careful about people we take on. If we find we have made a mistake, then we try to explain to the person concerned and try to part company amicably.'

It's also important that you do it properly. If the person in question is covered by the conditions necessary to claim unfair dismissal, you must make sure you follow the procedures. Being taken to the Industrial Tribunal is very time-consuming and expensive, even if you win.

There are basically two different scenarios when it comes to firing people. In the first, they've seen it coming. They're not happy, the job isn't what they'd expected, maybe they've even started looking somewhere else, and they're almost relieved when you make the decision. Those are comparatively easy to handle.

The other kind, where people simply haven't seen it coming, are much more difficult. We had someone here on trial some time ago, and when I called him in to say it wasn't working out, he thought I'd called him in to give him a rise. That's how far apart we were.

Those situations are messy and painful, and the temptation is to assuage your own feelings of guilt by laying all the blame on the person you're firing and telling her she was useless, idle, thick, disruptive, or whatever. But what you have to remember is that all you want is her job, not her self-respect, and though it's painful for you, it is much more painful for her. It doesn't hurt to take some of the responsibility on yourself – you made a mistake, you hadn't realized the job would grow as fast as it has, you thought she would fit in better with the existing staff . . . It is better that she leaves with her self-respect intact.

Ann Levick of Panmed Ltd says she still hasn't learnt to do it properly:

'My problem is that I leave it far too long. Instead of doing it months before in a calm, collected way, I wait till the final straw, when I'm at the end of my tether, and then do it in a rage. It is a weakness, but I am aware of it, and think that I can learn to do it better.'

Lois Jacobs finds it depends on the circumstance:

'If someone is not pulling their weight and is damaging the image of the company in which I take enormous personal pride, then I have no problem at all in firing them. Where it is difficult is when someone is giving their all, but just isn't up to it. You can try to find them something else within the company, or if not, you have to try to make them believe they want to go.'

Christina Smith finds it so difficult that she rarely does it:

'It has been said more than once, "Oh, go and work for Christina. She never fires anyone!" It's better if people leave – it does happen that people decide to go just as I'm plucking up the courage to say that the time has come to go our separate ways.

'With some people, the pay-off helps, but with others it doesn't. The shock of being fired isn't necessarily a bad thing. I know when it's happened to me that after the initial scream of pain, I have responded very constructively. But unfortunately, people who don't measure up to a job often don't respond in that way, and then I think you must let them off the hook as gently as possible. You never say, "You are no good".'

Customers

The other group of people without whom no business can exist – whether it's a multi-national or a one-woman band – is customers. Some people, I know, see them as an irritating interruption to the smooth-running of a business – you've just got all your knitwear neatly folded and stacked and along comes this customer who actually wants to take it out and look at it! But the simple fact is, without them you are sunk.

Obviously, before you even start a business, you must have a pretty good idea of who your customers are likely to be, even if the definition is pretty wide. I like to think Pineapple customers are people with great style! Christina Smith agrees:

'People often ask me which market I'm aiming at, and I usually say "The people who like my product", which a marketing person doesn't find very satisfactory. With shops and restaurants especially, you can't choose your customers, you don't know who's going to walk through your door. What I serve in the restaurants and what I sell in the shops are things I like. That's partly why you do it in the first place – because you as a consumer don't like what other people are doing. And you have to hope there are enough people who like what you do.'

I don't think it's possible for women to run a business in any other way. To say 'I don't like it but *they* will' is asking for trouble because you can't be totally committed and, when the chips are down, you can't just plain keep going unless you really love what you do. For most men, I think it is different. Power and money can motivate them and it doesn't matter whether they're producing baby powder or bulldozers!

But while backing your own taste is important, you must be commercial too. It's no good sitting in a shop or warehouse full of things you are passionate about, complaining that no-one wants to buy them. If you think that everything that people are buying at the moment is awful, then you're in the wrong business.

You must also accept that you can't please everybody, and can't be all things to all customers. If your hairdressing salon sets out to attract the ultra-trendies, you won't get many OAPs in for their blue rinses. I often think if we satisfied all the demands people make of us at Pineapple, we'd be producing a range of overalls too!

The joy of running your own small business is that you can be very close to your customers, get feedback from them and respond very quickly to their needs. As your business grows, that can become more difficult, but it is very important not to lose that close-to-the-customer feeling, so make sure there is good communication between you and your sales people.

At one time, we had a system whereby the people working in the shops would write down in a book anything customers asked for that we didn't have – a particular kind of tap shoe for example. Now we sell less specialist dancewear and much more fashion that doesn't apply in quite the same way, but I do get reports all the time – this isn't selling for the following reasons/this is too expensive/we can't get enough of these/we need a larger size in that.

EDUCATING THE CUSTOMER

Anita Roddick cares deeply about Body Shop customers and respects their intelligence. Unlike the long-established giants of the beauty business, Anita isn't interested in selling customers dreams and mystery. She is interested in educating them, explaining what the ingredients in Body Shop products are and what they do. Honesty has always been one of Anita's watchwords, and in the beginning it was a necessity. Having gambled £1,000 she could ill afford on a range of herbal products, she realized that the only way of selling a henna cream shampoo that looked like sludge and smelt like manure, was to explain to customers exactly what was in it and why it was good for their hair!

Anita is also passionate about raising the status of retailing in this country. Not only has she set up her own training school for staff, the company has sponsored a Chair in Retail Management for five years at Brighton Polytechnic, and she would love to open a museum of retailing. She encourages Body Shop assistants to see their job as giving information not selling:

'I don't want housekeepers in my shops. If a girl is dusting shelves when she could be talking to a customer, she should be working in a hotel or at home!'

'SEND THIS GUY THE FLEA LETTER . . .'

There's a story – apocryphal probably – about a man who wrote an angry letter to a railway company, after an overnight journey in a sleeper during which, he complained, he had been bitten by fleas. He received back the most grovelling letter of apology: how mortified the company was, how they had never had a complaint like this before and how they would make sure it never ever happened again. Unfortunately, attached to it by a careless secretary was his own letter of complaint with the handwritten words scrawled across it 'Send this guy the flea letter . . .'.

In ten years, I'm proud to say that while we've had lots of fan mail and very few letters of complaint, every department knows they must send any complaining letters to me because I feel so strongly about customer relations.

Luella Tills of Luella Windows Ltd., always sends flowers to customers if for some reason their order is delayed:

'Things do go wrong from time to time and sending flowers is my way of saying I'm sorry for the delay and that I do care. People appreciate it.'

'KEEP SMILING'

But like anyone for whom you feel affection, customers can also drive you mad. They'll come rushing in, saying their handbag's been stolen. They'll swear that they left it in the changing room, create havoc and then discover it had been in the studio all the time. They'll have out half the goods in the shop, and want the only style you don't have left in a particular colour. I do know how frustrated the shop staff can get, but I try to instil into them, 'Keep smiling!'

I remember the first really difficult customer we had at Covent Garden. She complained about absolutely everything, nothing was right and I was rather surprised that she became a 'regular'. After a while, she apologized for the way she'd behaved at the beginning. She had split up with her husband the week before, was living in a flat by herself, and since she'd found it too much to cope with, she'd taken it out on other people.

That taught me a valuable lesson and I pass it on to the people who work in the studios and the shops. Don't take it personally. If a customer is rude or difficult, just think 'Maybe she's had a row with her husband. Maybe her child's not well.' Always water it down and don't let your ego get in the way. If you do, you won't be able to handle it and the whole thing escalates into an unpleasant scene and that mars everyone's day.

Customers wholesale

The relationship with wholesale customers – shops and stores all over the country – should basically be the same, but if I'm honest I have to admit it can be quite difficult. If business in a shop is slow, the retailer may claim that your order arrived late and send it back, when in fact it arrived on time. One Christmas, a shop in Hull ordered some party dresses from us in three colours, the black and the red to be delivered first and the blue a week or so later. The factory making these dresses burnt down and as it was a specialized dress based on a tutu we couldn't find another manufacturer in this country in time. Not wanting to let our customers down, we resorted to using people I knew in Australia who rushed them through – we had to airmail the net for the dresses from here as they couldn't get it in Australia. It actually cost us more than the wholesale price we had quoted per dress but we honoured the original price as we were so keen to offer a good service and not let anyone down. As it happened, the blue and black arrived in our warehouse first, so we sent them off to the shop in question. The retailer went berserk, sent the whole lot back – black as well – even though the red ones would be arriving any day, saying we had ruined their window display plans. We refer to this moment in the history of Pineapple as 'death of wholesale!'

It's not unknown for retailers even to pull the seams of garments apart and then send them back saying they're faulty. It doesn't happen too often, fortunately, so you try not to be too cynical.

The nature of wholesaling is changing too. What used to happen was that people would see your samples, and then place an order which your supplier would make up. Obviously, it all takes a long time, and as fashion is changing so fast, some retailers are becoming reluctant to do that. What they want to do is order from stock, so they can have the clothing right away.

At the autumn Fashion Fair in London in October 1987 we had a buyer from Galeries Lafayette in Paris on the stand. She loved the whole collection, but instead of placing her order then for delivery in January or February, she said she wanted to come in February, and place an order for delivery in March. Since the cotton lycra fabric we use for a lot of our clothes takes at least twelve to fourteen weeks from the date of ordering, and it takes another three to four weeks to make it up, the only way we could meet her order was by having the garments in stock. It's very expensive to have a lot of money tied up in stock, not to say risky. In the old days, retailers took some of the risk themselves, but now they want us to take it all.

I said to Jeff Banks at the time, how clever he was having his own chain of shops and not having all the problems of wholesaling. He said, 'I woke up to that one ten years ago!'

By the end of 1987 we had decided that we would drop wholesaling and concentrate on licensing, mail order and retailing. Selling through our own shops meant that we could respond much more quickly to fashion trends. We could design garments and have them on sale in shops in just over six weeks. If deliveries of a particular line were late for whatever reason, we could simply put in more of something else. We would also have control over how the clothes were displayed and if they didn't sell we'd only have ourselves to blame!

When your business starts to take off, I think it's important to ask yourself every day whether you are doing what you want to do or whether you are spending a lot of time on something that's not fulfilling. You have to ask yourself as you go along, 'Am I enjoying myself?' And where wholesaling is concerned, the answer for me had to be 'No!'

As Noel Coward said, 'Work is more fun than fun', so you have to make sure it stays that way.

private lives

Perhaps the main difference between businessmen and businesswomen – still – is that many of us have to run not only our business but also a family and a home. No matter how much more widely accepted it is for women to work full-time, there is no doubt that when the chips are down – there's no loo paper left or a child has measles – the ultimate responsibility rests with us. It may be unfair but that's the reality.

So far we have concentrated on your career but you cannot separate your private life from your working life. You must not forget how important it is to organize your private life with the same degree of seriousness as you give to organizing your career. Otherwise you could end up being pulled in so many directions that you won't be able to cope.

Of course, things are much easier since the arrival of modern electrical appliances, laundries, prepared foods, delivery services, disposable nappies and so on, but even so it must be organized efficiently.

I have great admiration for Helen Gurley Brown. Her first book *Sex and the Single Girl* was an inspiration to me after my first marriage broke up when I was twenty, not only convincing me that there was life after divorce, but teaching me how to cook perfect fried eggs! Her second book *Having It All*, twenty or so years later, made me think, when I was debating whether to open a Pineapple in New York or not, that it really was worth going for it, flat out. But I do think its title, along with the title of Shirley Conran's book *Superwoman* shouldn't be taken too literally. Most of us can never be 'Superwoman' and we can't 'have it all'.

What you can have is *some* of all of it, and provided you are willing to accept that compromises will have to be made, you can keep your sanity into the bargain. Again, it's a question of priorities, of deciding what really matters to you and what you can survive without.

Kicking the guilt

One of the most difficult problems for women in business is the inbred feelings of guilt about not being the perfect mother, wife, mistress, housekeeper, laundress, cook, hostess and so on. Personally I haven't had too much of a problem with guilt partly because of my upbringing in Manchester. I was brought up in a very happy home and both my parents always worked. My mother did clerical work and my father had a plumbing contracting business. My mother enjoyed her job so much that I think she would still have done it even if she spent all her salary on bus fares and the cleaning lady. So as I was used to having a working mum, I couldn't understand why other girls' mothers stayed at home. I certainly didn't miss out in any way and in fact I became more mature for my age, having independence and responsibility from an early age. And since my father automatically shared the chores, I didn't discover male chauvinism until later in life!

Coping with the opposition

If your partner is against you setting up your own business, there's no doubt it is much more difficult. I am always being asked by women facing this dilemma what they should do. Often they are seriously considering giving up their plans because they are frightened that their marriage will break up if they go ahead.

But it seems to me that marriage is such a risky business that there are no guarantees anyway. If you don't start your business or take a job because your husband doesn't want you to, you are likely to feel frustrated and resentful which can be very destructive in a relationship. And even if you don't feel that way, you can't guarantee that he won't run off with his secretary anyway. The number of men whose second wives were once their secretaries is astonishingly high!

When I was married the first time, to a photographer, I had the chance of a film part. But it would have meant being away from home, living in London for some time, and my husband wasn't keen, so, thinking that my marriage was the most important thing, I turned it down. Not long after, he went off on an assignment and didn't bother to come home. So there I was at twenty with my first marriage finished anyway.

My advice would be if you think you can do it, then you must have a go. It will obviously be much tougher for you than it would be if you had your partner's full support and it will mean you have to try to allay the fears behind his opposition. If he's frightened of losing his comfortable, well-run domestic set-up, you have to learn to cut corners, to cheat, to buy help. If he's frightened of the fact that you will no longer be totally dependent on him financially and emotionally, point out the advantages for both of you – such as a happier, more fulfilled you, more disposable income in the family, even possibly a chance for him to ease off a little or take a career gamble that he would otherwise have been unable to consider.

CATCH 22

It's often said when a successful woman's marriage ends in divorce that the time and commitment she gave to her career was the cause. It's just not as simple as that – marriages break up for many reasons – the divorce rate is as high as one in 2.3 in London and I can assure you that if your marriage is a little unstable, staying at home to do the chores won't save it.

As more and more women are going into business it's getting confusing for some men as they are not sure what they want from a partner. There's no point therefore in asking them what they want you to do because one minute they're complaining about you not contributing financially, and then, when you are, they don't like you to put your career first.

Basically you can't win, so you must do what you feel is right for you. Things do go wrong in life – not just divorce but your partner could lose his job, become ill or even die, and at least if you have a career you can support yourself and your children.

When my father had a serious illness for many

months and had to give up his business, the job that my mother had always done because she enjoyed it became their major source of income.

Partners at home, partners at work?

Opinion varies sharply as to whether starting a business with your partner is a good idea or not. Certainly for some women it works spectacularly well. Sophie Mirman and her husband Richard Ross have made a huge success of the Sock Shop chain, and thoroughly enjoy working together:

'We share an office and we usually drive into work together, so we do try to make it a rule not to talk business all the time. We don't always succeed, though. If we see someone wearing a pair of our socks or tights (Richard says he now has the perfect excuse for looking at girls' legs without getting his wrists slapped!) or carrying a Sock Shop bag, we do break the rule. After all, we're both still so excited about it all that it's more like a hobby than work!'

Even though Anita Roddick's husband, Gordon, was riding horseback from Buenos Aires to New York when she opened the first Body Shop, he was involved in the business, albeit at long distance, from the start. He somehow managed to do the VAT returns sitting in a Brazilian jungle and as soon as he came back from his adventure, he took over the financial side of the business:

'I don't know how people can't work with their husbands! I love it! Gordon is the unsung genius of the company and he is such a terrific source of support. If I think I'm really useless, he'll back me up. If there's a problem, then I'm brilliant at talking it out with him. If you talk about a problem long enough you become so bored with it that it isn't a problem any more!'

If you are working together, it's probably best if you have separate areas of responsibility. Certainly, Sophie Mirman and Richard Ross have found that to be the case:

'I suspect that is why it works so well! Richard looks after the property side and the finances – he is an accountant after all – and I look after buying and design. Jointly, we oversee a number of other areas – personnel, the corporate side and so on.'

Other women prefer to go it alone, but with the support of their husbands. Pippa Gee, of Chambers International Products, decided to start her business because she had met her husband, a lawyer, in Staffordshire and, having previously worked abroad, had to find something to do locally:

'He is very interested in the business and I can always talk things over with him. He's behind me all the way – if he hadn't been I couldn't have done it. I couldn't have coped with a bad atmosphere.'

When Sophie Mirman won the Veuve Clicquot Businesswoman of the Year Award in 1988, her husband Richard Ross made the very astute comment 'Behind every successful businesswoman, there's a man without a chip on his shoulder!' (Not that Richard was implying that there had to be a man there at all!)

If the man in your life does have a chip about your

success, then you must be prepared to massage his ego. Don't hog the conversation when you're with friends or colleagues. Of course you're excited about what you're doing and want to tell everyone who's willing to listen, but make sure you balance that by asking his advice on subjects he is experienced in or where you value his opinion.

Just because you become used to making unilateral decisions at work, don't start doing the same at home, even if it is your money you're spending. If you've always made decisions jointly, then carry on doing so. My experience is that, if you do get on with your life, most men will respect you for it. Even though they may moan about it, most husbands will be very proud of the fact that their wives are successful.

Many younger men – though by no means all – have looked after themselves at some time in their lives so they are able to cook, clean, iron, shop. But if you haven't worked for some time and your husband is used to your being at home, you can't bring about a revolution overnight. You can't say, 'We're both working now, so you've got to take responsibility for half of the domestic chores.' If he's never helped with the shopping or cooking, he's unlikely to change just because you've started working. Of course he should be encouraged to do his bit – that's only fair – but you can't expect miracles and you'll run into trouble if you do.

The home front

When it comes to organizing your home, the two most important things to remember are, first, that you can't do it all, so decide on your priorities, and, second, that your time is very valuable. Most women, especially when they're starting out in their own business, or even in a job, never sit down and put a price on their own time. If you are worth £20 an hour to your business, how can it possibly be extravagant to pay someone £3 an hour to clean your house or do the family ironing?

Logically, it does make sense, but employing people to do what many women still believe, deep down, they ought to do for themselves, creates all sorts of guilt problems. As Anita Roddick puts it:

'I came home the other night to an empty house. The fridge was empty and there was mould in the breadbin. So I got out the can-opener, a tin of tuna, a tin of sweetcorn, the scrapings from the mayonnaise jar and a bit of chopped onion, mixed it up and ate it straight from the tin. I thought, "So this is what I've worked for forty years for! This is the epitome of success!"

'At present, someone comes in from our warehouse once a week to clean up the house, and that's it. I have set up a flat in the house for someone to live in and look after us, and ideally what I would like is someone who'd have the gin and tonic ready when I come in, fold all my clothes and put them away, prepare a delicious supper and then melt away. But the fact that I haven't even got round to looking for someone suggests that deep down I don't want to. Frankly, I'm too scared. I'm not used to all that and it makes me uncomfortable.'

And if you don't already feel guilt about it yourself, there's always someone who'll try to make you. I was interviewed by a journalist once who asked how I could possibly justify working and employing a cleaning lady and a nanny. How could I treat other women like servants, making them do my dirty work? My answer to that was 'Don't you have someone in your office who books your train tickets for you or gets you a cup of coffee?' You employ people at work to help you operate as efficiently as possible so why not at home? As long as you pay them a decent wage and *don't* treat them like servants, I really can't see that there's a problem.

THE CHORES

First of all, do a time and motion study on yourself, and see what takes up most of your time and how you could cut it down. Look at the style of your kitchen and living room. How much clutter is there that needs moving and dusting? Do you have a collection of brass or silver that needs regular cleaning? My home used to be full of antiques, knick-knacks and baskets of dried flowers, but now all that has gone. The apartment I had in New York when I was setting up Pineapple Broadway was all black and white, very simple with no clutter at all. I loved that kind of living, so I've adapted my home in London. All the clutter has been stored away. The only ornaments are huge pot plants, fresh flowers and candles. It's a look that is very right for now – hi-tech, minimalist – and it also has the huge advantage of being very easy to keep clean.

Finding a good cleaning lady is essential, though unless you find the paragon, again, you need to compromise. I've had cleaning ladies who were superb at cleaning, but who would never think of throwing out dead flowers or defrosting the fridge. I've had others who weren't so good at cleaning, but who would set the table beautifully if we were having people to dinner that evening, nip to the corner shop if we were out of anything and always pick some flowers or greenery from the garden and put them in a vase. On balance the latter suits me better, but if you're the type who worries about the odd smear on the shower screen or the top of a picture left undusted, then you'd probably find the former right for you. I've had a wonderful lady Josie helping me since my daughter Lara was a baby, and I don't know what I'd do without her.

Sophie Mirman has someone who comes in to do the housework every day, and sometimes when she is too busy to cook herself, a 'marvellous French woman' who comes in to do it for her.

If your cleaning lady comes a couple of times a week, she won't have time to do more than keep the house ticking over, so every six months or so you may want it springcleaned from top to bottom. There are now a number of agencies which provide such a service (most of them started by women), sending in a team, with all the necessary heavy duty equipment to do the job properly.

SHOPPING

Now that shops and supermarkets stay open much later in the evening, shopping isn't the problem it once was. I'm not alone in wondering what I did before discovering the delights of Marks and Spencer's food department! The quality is excellent and every time you pop in there seems to be something new to try.

However, I hate to do a regular weekly shop and as

time is of the essence I have found using local delivery services invaluable.

GET IT DELIVERED

I've managed to find a butcher, a fishmonger and a greengrocer who will take orders over the phone (our butcher even has a 24-hour answerphone so you can order the meat at midnight if you feel like it) and deliver the next day. We eat more fresh fruit and vegetables than anything else, so I keep a permanent list in my diary, and when I place an order I just run through and decide what we need. Of course it's more expensive than shopping in street markets and supermarkets, but the quality is first class, and again, your time is too valuable to waste on saving a few pence on a pound of tomatoes!

As for other things, most milkmen deliver dairy produce and eggs, and our butcher also has an excellent range of cheeses. Since we don't eat processed or canned food, that leaves only household items to shop for. Of course you need things delivered when your cleaning lady is there but if there's no-one at home, remember to ask them to put the delivery out of sight – it's a great invitation to burglars if they hang it on your front door, as I once found out!

Sophie Mirman quite enjoys the weekly shop:

'Shopping tends to be a Saturday morning job – three trolley loads from the supermarket! I can't really have stuff delivered because I don't quite know what I want until I see it, and besides, I actually find it quite interesting going round shops and seeing what's happening – how things are being packaged and marketed.'

FEEDING THE FAMILY

Since many women associate food with love – hence all the overweight children you see around – this is the area in which any guilt we feel about working comes bubbling to the surface! One woman who has started a very successful free newspaper in the north, for example, still insists on doing all the family baking herself – her way of salving her conscience. Many women still find the idea of getting a take-away supper hard to accept. However, there are lots of different styles of take-away these days, and an even greater time-saver are the delivery services which are now starting up in some cities – you order on the 'phone and half an hour later the food arrives piping hot. We use 'Dial-a-Meal' regularly for delicious Tandoori dishes or excellent Chinese food.

If you prefer to do the cooking yourself, life is also much easier now than it used to be. In the last few years, the range of prepared dishes available in supermarkets and chain stores has improved beyond all recognition. A few years ago, the family would complain, and quite rightly, if you dished up a TV dinner, but now the fish or chicken dishes are almost as good as home-made, especially as there has been a cutback in the use of food additives, salt and sugar.

The fresh pasta shops that have now opened in some towns are also a great help to working women. The different colours and shapes of pasta all take only a couple of minutes to cook and many shops also sell freshly-made sauces to go with them – not just the usual Bolognese or Napolitana, but all sorts of interesting concoctions of herbs and nuts, or vegetables. Keep a small piece of whole Parmesan in the fridge (the ready-grated stuff doesn't taste as good) to grate over it once it's cooked, and you have a gourmet meal in under five minutes.

ENTERTAINING

I find more often than not that entertaining, whether business or social, is easier done in restaurants. There are now so many good places to choose from in London and around the country, but I do still enjoy entertaining at home when I can. Even though I have very little time, it needn't take all day to prepare especially if you can manage to have the food delivered.

There are many simple starters such as fresh asparagus, avocados, pâtés, hummus and taramasalata with hot pitta bread, crudités, smoked salmon, watercress soup, ogen melons with the addition of a little port or with Parma ham to name but a few – all of which are easy to prepare in minutes.

Roasts and grills are always easy with jacket potatoes and fresh vegetables. In summer I love to do barbecues and it no longer takes forever to prepare the salad as ready-prepared ones are available, and dressings such as Paul Newman's and Marks and Spencer fresh French dressing are great when time is short.

I rarely serve puddings as most people nowadays are watching their weight and wouldn't thank you for a chocolate mousse or a bread and butter pudding, so I usually serve fresh fruit and a selection of cheeses. Yes, of course all these things are expensive – it seems that the cheaper the ingredients the longer you have to spend preparing them – but as we all know, time is money.

If you do want to have a large dinner party there are

lots of freelance cooks around, and if you don't know of any in your area an ad in the local paper might well give someone who's looking for a business to start a good idea.

Children

In spite of the huge strides that women have made in the last ten years or so, there is no doubt that for mothers who work the problems of child care are still a major, often limiting, factor.

While I was still modelling, it was comparatively easy. When Lara was very small, I could take her with me to the studio in her carrycot.

But in Anita Roddick's case her choice of what kind of business to start was dictated by the fact that she had two small children and a husband then half-way across South America on a horse:

'It is a lot easier to get started if you have no kids, or if you're already wealthy enough to afford a nanny, but I wasn't. So I had to think of something I could do with a six-year-old and four-year-old, and a mother willing to help out. After running a hotel and restaurant, which Gordon and I had been doing and which is a twenty-four hours a day, seven days a week job, a shop which was nine to five seemed perfect. Imagine the joy of locking the door behind me at a reasonable hour, picking up the kids from my mum's and going home!'

Steve Shirley of 'F International', the freelance computer consultancy company, started her hugely successful business from home because she wanted to bring up her children herself:

'I had a babysitter one afternoon a week, and made all my appointments for that afternoon. I'd say "I've got a very busy week, but I could make Tuesday afternoon." Later on, if I had a family commitment on a particular day, I would never say so. I'd simply say I wasn't free that day.'

I also believe that it is very important not to let family life *appear* to interfere with your work.

Sophie Mirman was already running a very successful business when her daughter Natasha was born, and she knew there was no way she could give up work and stay home full-time:

'Ten days after Natasha was born, I was itching to get back to work so back I came. With William, born eighteen months later, it was the same. I adore them and would do anything for them, but I think I love them more being able to continue with my career and work normally, than I would staying at home looking after them full-time.'

For a lot of women, though, as we have said, guilt is a huge problem – guilt that you are being selfish, that your children are suffering because you are working. Anita Roddick found it an enormous problem:

'I dealt with it by buying them brilliant presents every time I went away – it was as stupid as that! I stopped doing this a couple of years ago when I sussed that they only wanted all this stuff to impress their friends, not for themselves.'

Feelings of guilt are something that other people – relatives, acquaintances, other non-working mothers –

are only too happy to fuel. Any problems your child may have, from a runny nose to dyslexia, are blamed on the fact that you're a working mother. Dinah Jane Ladenis, who works with her husband Nico in their restaurant, was told that her daughter's learning difficulties were due to the fact that she had chosen to follow her husband instead of being a mother!

Even the professionals have joined in. John Bowlby's famous book *Attachment and the Growth of Love* stressed the importance of the mother's constant presence in the early years, and various studies suggested that children whose mothers worked did less well than those who didn't. But then it turned out that most of those studies were done on children who were in day nurseries or with childminders because there was deprivation or other problems in the family. However, an intensive survey, conducted by Professor Neville Butler of YOUTHSCAN, which is soon to be published, has now shown that children under five who had working mothers did just as well as those whose mothers were with them full time, as long as their caretakers (nannies, sitters, au pairs, etc.) were satisfactory. And in fact, children from happy families whose mothers worked and who were cared for by a permanent mother-substitute did better than average because they were given undivided attention all day and didn't have to share it with the housework, the shopping, the cooking and the ironing.

One of my friends was very hard on me because I went back to work when Lara was a baby. Before she was twelve months old Lara could walk and talk and was very bright. On the other hand my friend's baby couldn't talk and had also had tests for deafness. The baby was found to be normal but they discovered the cause of the problem was that her mother was so immersed in the chores that she never chatted to her baby. Meanwhile Lara was getting quality rather than quantity and concentrated stimulation (I even used the controversial 'Teach your Baby to Read' flashcards from six months), because after going to work I so enjoyed my time with her.

SUBSTITUTE MUMS

For the sake of your children, and for your own peace of mind, you must provide the best possible substitute care that you can find. If you are just starting out and money is tight so that you can't really afford to pay for full-time help, then a mother or mother-in-law living nearby can be a life-saver. But remember, while grannies are thrilled to see their grandchildren for a few hours, full-time care of a small child is exhausting. It's tiring enough when you're thirty, never mind when you're sixty or seventy.

There are day nurseries (as opposed to nursery schools whose very short hours mean they don't offer a solution for working mothers) but state-run ones give priority to children from problem families and single-parent families whose mothers have to work, and private ones, if you can find them, are quite expensive. There are childminders, of course, and some of them are very good. Again, asking around is probably the best way of finding one. But if they live some distance away, taking and collecting your child can make it a very long day indeed for both of you. Remember too that using a childminder won't be the answer if you're regularly delayed by crises at work and turn up late to collect your child – it's inconvenient for the childminder and, more importantly, may upset the child's bedtime routine.

If you can afford it, then a nanny is probably the answer. Some people think of au pairs as an alternative, but they aren't always. They are foreign girls who are supposed to live as part of the family, to do only light household duties and to have time off in the day for language classes. They won't necessarily have experience of caring for small babies, and if you are planning to leave someone in sole charge of your child, you need to have total confidence that she knows what she's doing. For slightly older children who are learning to talk, spending all day with someone whose English is not a great deal better than their own hardly qualifies as the best possible substitute care, either.

If you decide that a nanny is the answer, the next problem is finding a good one. Given that there are so many women working now, there are more jobs looking after children than good nannies to fill them, so it's not as easy as it was when I was looking, twelve or thirteen years ago.

Sophie Mirman has had the same marvellous nanny since Natasha was born and knows how lucky she is – in fact she touches wood every time she talks about her!

HOW TO FIND A NANNY

The best way of finding a good nanny is to put the word around on the local nanny network – someone already working in the area may be looking for another job. If so, she will know her way around, already have an established circle of friends and be likely to settle in much more quickly than someone coming from out of town.

One of the popular ways of finding nannies is to advertise in *The Lady* magazine as Sophie Mirman did. Before you place your ad, it's worth buying a copy to see the sort of wording used, and to see the competition you're up against. Don't be depressed by the occasional ad that offers a self-contained flat, a smart car for the nanny's sole use, two months in Marbella every year and £150 a week. There are only a few of those and, besides, most experienced nannies know there is almost always a catch – working seven days a week, twenty-four hours a day and being treated like a skivvy for example! Given that it is a competitive market, you have to sell yourself and exploit everything you have going for you. If you have an exciting career then say what you do in your ad. If you live in an attractive area, say so.

AGENCIES

There are also lots of nanny agencies, who, like all employment agencies, vary in price (charging fees from £200–£350 for finding a permanent nanny) and in quality. Some make you feel that unless you're offering the self-contained flat, smart car and holidays in Marbella, you are wasting their time. Others send you nannies who are exactly what you said you didn't want – inexperienced, unqualified girls when you wanted an NNEB (a nanny holding the Nursery Nursing Education Board's qualification) with at least two years' experience. But some are very good, and worth every penny.

Interviewing potential nannies requires the same skills as interviewing any staff with the additional factor that, since they will be sharing your home, you have to be able to live with them as well. Inevitably it has to be a compromise – you might have to settle for someone who is great with children but is fiendishly untidy and can do little more than boil an egg. You can't really tell what someone is like until she is living with you, so it has to be a question of trial and error. If it doesn't work out, then don't mind getting rid of someone and trying again even though it's a hard and time-consuming business.

There is an element of luck involved, too. I had nine nannies in the first eighteen months – one left because her mother became ill, another couple were so untidy I couldn't stand it, another was a manic depressive and so on – and then one came along who stayed till Lara was six. If you do have bad luck, just keep on trying. Eventually the right person will turn up and, for the peace of mind you get from having total confidence in her, it's worth all the aggravation.

Going to school

Once your children reach school age, the problems aren't any easier, they're just different. If they're at school from 9 a.m. till 3.30 p.m. you don't really need a full-time nanny, but you do need someone to collect them from school and be there in the holidays. Some people find au pairs ideal in this situation because they can fit in their classes during the day while the children are at school, and they tend to have holidays at the same time too. Once the children are older, they can go off on outings together that they'll all enjoy.

BOARDING SCHOOLS

In many ways, boarding school is an attractive solution for working mothers, but it's by no means right for every child. I was lucky in that Lara actually wanted to be a boarder.

When she was six, we bumped into some friends whose daughter had left Sibton Park, a prep. school in the country, that day and was devastated about leaving because she had had such a wonderful time there. I took Lara to see it and it really was fabulous – a lovely old manor house set in beautiful countryside and run by a delightful couple. They didn't then take children until they were seven, but Lara was so impressed by what she saw that she asked if she could start that Friday! After some informal tests, the head said she was bright enough to start, but he was concerned that she might not be ready emotionally. He made the very good point that if you do try boarding school before the child is ready, you will probably have ruined your chances of making it work later on. He suggested that Lara went initially as a weekly boarder. On the way home, we discussed it, and Lara was adamant that she didn't want to come home at weekends. She had been talking to the other girls there and they'd told her the weekly boarders missed all the fun at weekends.

Lara started full-time at Sibton in the September before her seventh birthday. When I rang her up after the first couple of days and asked how she was she said cheerfully, 'I'm homesick!' I said, 'Oh are you? What does that mean?' She said 'I don't know but everybody here gets it!' She loved Sibton so much that when I took her to the school bus after half-term, she could hardly even be bothered to wave goodbye.

I dreaded how she would take the transition from Sibton to a senior boarding school. I called in a schools expert, Nicki Archer, who knows about all the independent schools. She meets your child, sees her school reports and suggests several schools that she thinks might be right for her. You can't just rely on recommendations from friends with children, because what might have suited theirs down to the ground might not be right for yours. It is fairly time-consuming driving round the countryside to visit all these schools, but it is time well invested.

Atmosphere was what I was looking for and the only way you can assess that is by going to the school. One school I looked at had a very bitchy atmosphere; in another, the place was a mess, and it was clear the discipline had gone. I then took Lara to three that I'd liked, and the moment she walked into Westonbirt she couldn't wait to move there. It also helped that a close friend of Lara's was already at the school. It is terribly important to get the choice of school right. If your child is unhappy or isn't doing well, then you are faced with all the upheaval of moving them mid-stream, which is unsettling for them and worrying for you.

Anita Roddick managed to juggle business and her children's schooling with the help of her mother – but only just:

'When we moved into our present house in the country five years ago, they were at school next to our warehouse complex, but I felt like a wire being stretched. My mum was helping with the kids, but being a typically indulgent Italian grandma she wasn't making them do their homework, and was filling their faces with junk food. And they hated the country because they were twelve and thirteen and there was no-one their own age in the village nearby. So, after much heart-searching, we decided to send them as weekly boarders to a progressive boarding school. They both loved it! Children have no right to be so happy! It meant that Gordon and I could get on during the week, without feeling guilty about them, and they were pleased to see us at weekends.'

If your children are at boarding school, you are still left with the problem of what to do in the holidays, especially as they are longer than day school holidays. I found students were ideal because they are usually very bright. We had an American girl once who was great and full of energy. She'd pack up a picnic lunch and take Lara off to do the sights. It's a good idea to put up a notice in the students' union of the local college or place an ad in the student newspaper.

Health

It's one of life's great clichés, I know, but your health is the most precious gift you have. Without it, life becomes very difficult. I became acutely aware of this over twenty years ago when I developed a condition known as hypo-thyroidism, which meant my thyroid was underactive, and my weight suddenly shot up from around eight stone to over eleven. And as you can imagine, the career prospects for a size eight model who has put on three stone are strictly limited. The conventional doctors I consulted gave me no hope, with advice that ranged from 'it's an incurable condition' to 'you will lose weight as soon as you stop eating'. Since

I was eating hardly anything, that advice seemed particularly callous and unhelpful.

ALTERNATIVE MEDICINE

Having found no help at all from conventional medicine, I started to explore alternative therapies and eventually a friend of mine, writer and film director David Leland, introduced me to Dr Chandra Sharma, a homeopath who, without exaggeration, changed my whole life. Not only did he introduce me to homeopathy and a healthy wholefood diet (remember this was twenty years ago, when even eating brown bread was thought to be rather eccentric), he also recommended dance as the ideal exercise.

I have been a firm believer in homeopathy ever since. In twenty years I haven't even taken an aspirin. When I had an operation to remove a ruptured appendix and a huge ovarian cyst, soon after Lara was born, I insisted on homeopathic injections afterwards instead of penicillin. Although the nurses were all very worried that I would get an infection, I recovered so quickly that I was home within five days.

Once you've learnt the basics of homeopathy, you can have a medicine chest at home and treat yourself very easily. Even if you've got the wrong remedy, it can't do you any harm.

YOU ARE WHAT YOU EAT

Dr Sharma also introduced me to a much healthier diet. I gave up white bread, white sugar, fried food, anything out of a can – he believed that canned food was dead food – and all 'junk'. Instead I eat fresh food – lots of vegetables, salads and fruit, fish, chicken and meat. I did give up red meat altogether for a while but, as I've since found that I can fit it into my diet, I will have a steak occasionally.

I'm not fanatical about diet – that in itself is unhealthy. If I find myself in a situation where all that's on offer is a sausage sandwich made with soggy white bread, so what? I'll eat it, and I love the occasional fish and chips.

I cook in stainless steel, copper or enamel pans. Dr Sharma believed that some aluminium and non-stick pans, as well as aluminium foil, make the food neurotoxic.

Dr Sharma also persuaded me to give up caffeine. Caffeine affects homeopathic remedies and therefore must be avoided when you are having treatment. It's also a severe nerve stimulant and some people don't break it down and are badly affected, as it makes them feel tense and irritable. I must admit I feel much better without it and drink herb teas (Jill Davies has a wonderful selection with names like 'Morning Starter' and 'Evening Peace') but I do have the occasional cappuccino which I love.

ALCOHOL AND CIGARETTES

As we all know, alcohol and smoking are bad for your health – artificially stimulating to the nervous system and highly toxic, not to mention the risks of cancer. I avoid smoking but I do enjoy wine and champagne (I never drink spirits). I don't drink at lunchtime and try to stick to Dr Sharma's philosophy of everything in moderation!

Survival of the fittest

There is no doubt that running a business, running a home, and bringing up children is tough, and you can't expect much sympathy from anyone. So you will need every bit of stamina – and sanity – you can get. And there is also no doubt that regular exercise does increase your stamina and also your ability to handle stress.

You can say it's all right for me to talk about regular exercise – I have a Pineapple Studio on my doorstep. It's not only important for me personally to keep fit, but I do have a certain image to keep up and if I were seen to be getting flabby, it wouldn't be very good for business!

It's not realistic to suggest that you should find time to exercise every day – unless you could cycle to work – but everybody can find the time to do something a couple of times a week.

Try to find something that's fun and arrange to go with a friend. You're much more likely to go regularly if you go with someone else, so you can nag each other and stop any backsliding.

GIVE YOURSELF A BREAK

Exercise is very valuable in managing stress, something we all suffer from though it's often difficult to recognize and own up to. You say 'I'm okay. My shoulders are down, not up round my ears, so I can't be feeling stressed.' But there are other signs. When I find I'm taking longer than I used to to decide what to put on in the morning, or when I'm making a phone call and I can't remember who I'm phoning, I know that the stress level is up. For me the answer then is a weekend away or a week or so at a health farm like Shrublands. I think the chance to cleanse your system thoroughly and have a complete rest is absolute bliss. It costs about the same as a week's package holiday in Greece, and the benefits are incalculable. Within a matter of days, you can see the stress disappearing from people's faces. When they arrive, they're so tense they don't speak to anyone and they just bury their noses in a book. By the third or fourth day they're smiling and saying 'Hello, how are you getting on?'

Ann Levick has found that time to be alone has become increasingly important:

'I write in my diary at least two evenings a week "IN". If you're with people all day, you need desperately to be on your own sometimes. I'm out of the age group – thank God – where you think you have to be out Friday and Saturday night or else you're a social failure. For me, Friday night is the best night of the week. I collapse on the sofa, feet up, with a glass of wine in my hand and the weekend stretching ahead of me!'

It is terribly important to stand back, not just once a year, but as often as you can, and look at your life. It's all too easy just to get carried along by what you're doing.

The best laid plans . . .

No matter how well-organized you may be, you simply cannot legislate for disaster striking. Early in 1984, Lara's school rang to say she was complaining of a pain in her left shoulder and she was losing the strength in her left hand. An ambulance rushed her to London, and at 4 a.m. at the Maudsley Hospital they told me they suspected a spinal tumour, and had to operate right away otherwise she might not live. I wanted a second opinion, but was accused of being neurotic and endangering her life, and so against my instincts I gave in. There was no tumour, but she came out of the operation paralysed from the neck down.

The Maudsley just wasn't geared to care for children and when they decided they wanted to operate again, Dr Sharma – who had been certain from the beginning that there was no tumour – had Lara moved to Great Ormond Street. It was terribly overcrowded and I had to sleep in a chair by her bed for several nights, until they found a camp bed for me, but the nurses were absolutely wonderful.

However, Great Ormond Street also decided another operation was necessary. Dr Sharma felt that it was best to take Lara home immediately and to start treating her homeopathically. The atmosphere at the hospital had been so negative – people coming in to examine her, then tut-tutting and shaking their heads – and he felt it was vital to get her home into a positive atmosphere.

When we got her home, Dr Sharma put Lara on a very strict vegetarian diet, with nothing from a packet or tin, and she had regular massage and physiotherapy. The physiotherapist was reluctant when she first heard about the case, as she believed Lara ought to be in hospital. On her first visit Lara swore and cursed at her, and I was mortified. I walked to the door with her and apologized for Lara's behaviour, but she said, 'It's great that she's so angry! We spend months trying to get patients to react positively like that. Now I feel there really might be a chance.'

A number of top neurologists saw Lara, and the message we got from all of them was the same – that there was no hope and that if more surgery was recommended that's what she should have. I finally asked one of them whether the operation would enable her to walk again, and he said, 'Oh no. The surgery will save her life because the paralysis is creeping inward. After surgery she'll definitely be paraplegic, if not quadraplegic, but she'll live.'

When they had taken her away for that first opera-tion, I felt that I'd done the wrong thing in agreeing and I made a pledge to myself that if she survived I wouldn't be persuaded by anyone to do anything that I didn't feel was right, that I would trust my instinct. And that's what I did. If she had the second operation, there was no chance at all that she would recover. If she didn't have it, there was a chance she might recover, so I believed we had to go that route. I told the neurologist this and he accepted it but said if we ever needed him, we should call.

That weekend, Lara started to move her right leg. I phoned the neurologist on Monday and told him what had happened. He said, 'The child I saw on Friday had no possibility of ever moving her leg. You carry on doing it your way and I'll come and see her whenever you like.'

There was so much positive feeling around. Dr Sharma never doubted for a minute that she would get better in spite of all the experts telling us there wasn't a chance. Without him, I know I couldn't have got through it.

Over the next few months, Lara gradually regained most of the use of her limbs. The right side came back before the left, and for quite a long time her left hand was pretty useless. But she worked incredibly hard and though she could never be 100%, she could be 99%.

Dr Sharma was wonderful and came to see Lara every day. Doctors later declared him 'the miracle man'. He was going through personal problems of his own at this time and was fighting for custody of his daughter Yamuna. Sadly in April 1986 he died of a heart attack. We miss him terribly but he will always be remembered with great affection by the many people he has helped over the years. His son Dr Rajendra Sharma had been working with him for some time and now carries on the practice very successfully.

In many ways, it was very lucky that I had my own business. It was clear from the moment that Lara came round from the operation paralysed, that it was going to take months and months to get her better. If I'd been working for someone else, I would have had to resign. As it was, I had people working for me to keep the business ticking over.

Of course, at the beginning I did think about giving it all up. We had just started building work on the new Pineapple Studios in New York and in South Kensington, and people did ask why I didn't just call a halt. But we had bought the New York building, we'd signed the lease in South Kensington, the builders had started in both places and it would have been much more difficult to stop than to carry on. Besides, I thought that it would be less dramatic for Lara if she saw life going on as normal around her. If I seemed suddenly to abandon everything, she might well have got the message that she really was seriously ill and I am a great believer in the power of thought, both positive and negative.

In fact Lara was very interested in what was going on. A dear friend, Mary McKenzie, stepped in to help at that time and took over the organization of the South Kensington studios. She used to come in the evenings and bring fabric swatches and paint colours to show us, and Lara would help choose them. Since she had been to New York the Christmas before she became ill, and had seen the building on Broadway, she was interested in what was happening there too.

The other major factor in my decision not to give up altogether was that Pineapple was by then a public company, and as the events of autumn 1987 showed only too clearly, in the City confidence is the key. If the word had got out that Pineapple plc had lost its chairman, our shares could well have nosedived. So during those first few months when I was at home with Lara, my PA would ring me with important messages, and I would call people back so that they needn't know that I wasn't in the office.

While Lara was still in hospital, I was due to collect the Variety Club Business Woman of the Year Award in the presence of HRH Prince Philip. I felt that if I didn't turn up the press might start asking questions, and the last thing I wanted for our sakes and for Pineapple's was Lara's illness becoming public knowledge. So, a friend of mine, David Fielden, an ex-dancer who makes beautiful evening wear, sent a ball gown to the hospital and I changed in Lara's room. She was thrilled about that and thrilled I was getting the award. I had a 'phone in the car in case the hospital rang and during the award ceremony the chauffeur stayed by the 'phone in the car. Afterwards, we drove straight back to the hospital.

Soon after this I won the Veuve Clicquot Business-woman of the Year Award and Lara was pleased to see it in all the papers, and enjoyed the giant pineapple-shaped cake the chef at the Institute of Directors had made specially for the occasion.

It was a very long slow process, but by September I felt Lara was ready to go back to school. She still wasn't completely better, her left side was still very weak, and she had got to the point where she was fed up with it all and couldn't be bothered to do her exercises any more. I believed that being with her friends and wanting to keep up would encourage her to make the progress she still needed to make. As it turned out it was just the motivation she needed and within weeks there was a definite improvement.

By the time Lara went back to school the following September, I was absolutely drained in one way and yet I'd wake up every morning full of inner elation, knowing how lucky we'd been. When your child has nearly been taken from you and a miracle has happened, nothing will faze you after you've lived through something like that. All the other problems you meet seem trivial by comparison, and easy to tackle, and though you are exhausted you find the energy to push on and try to catch up with your life. As far as Pineapple was concerned, there was a great deal of catching up to do, but more of that later.

Lara's illness recurs

Exactly four years later, in February 1988, I was in the office literally signing the papers that made Pineapple mine again, when someone from Lara's school phoned. She had collapsed while she was out riding and had been taken to the nearby Frenchay Hospital in Bristol. I rushed down there to find her paralysed again.

This time, though, Lara had a brilliant neuro-surgeon called Mr Coakham and as Frenchay Hospital has a Magnetic Resonance Imaging scanner (donated by a local businessman – John Adams) he was able immediately to diagnose the cause of the paralysis on both occasions as AVM (Arterial Venal Malformation). Basically there was a faulty artery inside her spinal column, which is very rare, and when it haemorrhaged it pressed on the spinal cord and paralysed her.

Mr Coakham drained the haemorrhage within hours but felt that the risks involved in attempting to repair the AVM, which was very close to the spinal cord, were too great. So again we did the rounds of doctors worldwide and eventually found that the specialist with the most experience of this difficult operation called embolization was Dr Berenstein, who worked at the New York University Medical Center.

It was a very difficult time. All the doctors I spoke to said that if the operation to close the faulty artery wasn't done then it could haemorrhage again at any time, causing progressively worse paralysis, if not death. If the operation was carried out, though, there was a risk that she could be paralysed permanently. What made the decision more agonizing was that after weeks of physiotherapy and sheer guts, Lara had begun to walk again with help. And the temptation to stick my head in the sand, do nothing and just hope that it would be all right was very strong.

Anyway, finally the decision was made, and Lara and I flew to New York in August 1988 for tests, and then the operation. It was an almost total success – much better than even the surgeon had hoped for. Two weeks later we flew home and Lara went back to school on 12 November 1988, the day after her fifteenth birthday.

Money can't buy health I know, but if I hadn't had my own business I could never have contemplated taking Lara to New York. There are people who say that the children of mothers with careers are deprived, but in this instance it was only because I worked that I was able to do the best for Lara.

Expanding

Move with the times

I used to have a saying, 'Every plan made is an opportunity lost!' because I felt that if you try to plan the way your business – indeed, your life – will go down to the last detail, you are no longer able to seize any opportunity that may arise unexpectedly. Some of my colleagues have always told me how unbusiness-like that was, so I was very pleased to read in his book, *The Art of the Deal*, that Donald Trump, the New York property-developing multimillionaire, operates in much the same way if not more so!

'I play it very loose. I don't carry a briefcase. I try not to schedule too many meetings. I leave my door open . . . I prefer to come to work each day and just see what develops.'

One real strength of small business is that because you are so close to your customers and because you don't have a huge, unwieldy corporate infrastructure, you can see what your customers want and respond to their needs very quickly.

Certainly in the early days, Pineapple expanded purely in response to demand. It became clear very soon after we opened that we needed more space, so we paid the photographer on the first floor £30,000 to move up to the second floor, which gave us space to create a big studio on the first floor which was badly needed for professional classes.

When we first opened, we had a tiny clothing shop on the ground floor next to the café. When we took over the first floor, we moved the café up there, and, in doing so, doubled the size of the shop, and doubled the take!

The demand for the clothing just grew and grew – people with shops were buying it at a 10% discount – so it became clear that the wholesale side of it was an obvious growth area, if we could find the space in which to do it.

The building next door was an old banana store that was being used as a shop and warehouse by Kobi Jeans. I got to know the people who ran it and asked them to let us have first refusal if ever they decided to move, and one day in 1981 I got a phone call to say that they were leaving and someone wanted to buy the lease for a wine bar. I had to move really fast. We had to complete the deal by eleven o'clock the next morning or else, by two o'clock that afternoon, it would have gone.

We got it, though I got myself into trouble with the accountants because there hadn't been time to prepare a proper business plan. We opened a bigger shop and not only doubled the take again but got the wholesale clothing operation under way at the same time.

Sometimes you have to break the rules and take a risk in business, or it can be a missed opportunity.

Going West (Our second centre)

Late in 1981 we had decided to open a second 'Pineapple'. We were already short of space and the teachers wanted more teaching hours which we simply couldn't offer them at Covent Garden, so I had started looking for a building.

On my way to work one day, I saw a 'To Let' sign in Paddington Street, just off Baker Street. I rushed into a rather small entrance hall which opened into a huge, wonderful airy studio space. I rang the landlords, the Howard de Walden Estates, from the payphone in the hall and said, 'I want it!' They said, 'So do five other people!' The people ahead of me included a carpet warehouse and a garage; however the secretary of the Estates office felt it would be a great service to the local community if Pineapple opened there, so luck was shining on me and we got the building.

ONE STEP AHEAD OF THE COMPETITION

We had to move at the speed of light to open Pineapple West before competitive studios started to open up, riding on the crest of the 'fitness boom' wave which had also just begun. Then I could say to my teachers, 'Now you've got two Pineapples to work in, you don't have to go elsewhere.' Obviously you can't say to people, 'If you go there, you can't work here any more.' Instead, you make them an offer they can't refuse.

But it was a very difficult time. My teachers were tempted by free studio space for a while, offered by a competitor, and then lower rents than I was charging. In fact seven of the teachers left to go elsewhere. Within a fortnight, five of the seven were back with us as things didn't turn out as they expected. One of our competitors also distributed leaflets in Covent Garden and took a full page ad on the back page of *The Stage* for several weeks offering free membership to Pineapple members.

Three more of my staff were lured away and naturally I really hated losing staff. I'd built up a nice little team and trained them so well they knew all the systems we'd developed for running a dance centre.

Having a second studio also gave me the strength to negotiate favourably with my clothing suppliers, and during this period, in fact, we didn't lose any suppliers at all.

There's an old story about a shopkeeper who finds one day that a shop selling exactly the same stock is opening opposite. He sees it all happening, sees the customers going in and out of his rival's shop all day long, and eventually says to a friend, 'I don't understand it. We sell the same things at the same prices, and yet he's doing so much better than I am.' His friend says, 'He's only worrying about one business. You're worrying about two!' There is a danger that you are so busy keeping an eye on the opposition that you're no longer running your own business properly. Obviously, you have to smarten up your act to stay ahead, but you mustn't be panicked into making changes simply as a response to what the opposition is doing.

SMALL, BEAUTIFUL . . . AND BANKRUPT

So in this instance, expanding was a question of survival. People have often said to me, 'Why did you have to grow so big? Why didn't you keep Pineapple the way it was in the beginning?' The answer to that is very simple. If I had kept it as it was, there would be no Pineapple now. I would have lost my teachers to bigger studios. When we started, we had just four small basement studios and two ground floor ones, and when large studios started opening up, loyalty alone wouldn't have kept them with us. You can't stand still in business, you have to keep moving forward or else the competition will come up and overtake you.

TWO STUDIOS ARE BETTER THAN ONE

I actually found it easier to run two places than one. One place didn't justify a book-keeper, so I did the books myself, but two places did. Now that I had two places to oversee, I no longer had time to mop the loos, or queue up at the bank, or collect the stock from the manufacturers – all the time-consuming jobs you have to do yourself in the beginning because you can't afford to pay people to do them for you. As you expand, you can't afford to do them yourself. Your working day gets more and more interesting because you can delegate much of the 'housework' and concentrate on developing the business.

New York, New York

I began to think I'd like a Pineapple in Paris, New York, even Tokyo. As for Paris, I did look for a suitable building but never found one. New York came about as the result of demand.

When we opened there, one city journalist in London wrote a very critical report saying I'd really blown it now, and that I was taking coals to Newcastle! But in fact, whenever American dancers were working in London and came to Pineapple to rehearse, or for class, they would say, 'You must open up in New York because we have nothing like this. We have smart, expensive health and racquet clubs, we have ballet studios here, jazz studios there, audition and rehearsal space somewhere else and a dancewear shop miles away, but nowhere that has everything in the same place.'

I found it hard to believe – after all, New York is the dance capital of the world – so I went over there, and found it was true. I met some people in the dance world there who were marvellous to me and I felt very quickly it would be an exciting thing to do. I love New York and it helps if you enjoy going to a place. In fact, a business friend of mine says he only opens branches in places he enjoys visiting, which makes sense. Certainly if you are thinking of expanding abroad, you have to ask yourself, 'Do I enjoy travelling?' If the answer is 'No I hate it', then think very hard indeed before you commit yourself.

Before I finally decided to expand to New York, I made a list – all the pluses in one column, all the minuses in the other – something I always do if I am in two minds about something. The minuses included the difficulty of finding the right building, finding an architect to work on it, finding somewhere to live, finding the right staff and of keeping control at long distance. The pluses were that there really was a demand for it, and I really wanted to do it!

As always, I put the word around everyone I knew that I was looking for a suitable building for studios. Late in 1983, my dear friend, June Summerill, rang me one day to tell me about a studio for sale in SoHo (an area in down-town New York), which was then still largely ungentrified. (The journalist who said I'd blown it by opening in New York also said I'd made a big mistake buying a building in such an unfashionable area!) I had a look, but it was much too small. The owner knew of another building nearby that he thought might be suitable, and took me there.

Pineapple Broadway – No. 3

That building wasn't right either, but next door to it was the perfect building. By then we had developed a nine-point check list for potential studios, and this building scored a perfect nine! It was 200 feet long and 40 feet wide, with no pillars to break up the floor space, and windows on three sides, so the natural daylight was superb.

The other problems somehow resolved themselves. Again, by asking around, I found a marvellous apartment. As for someone to run the studios, Steven Giles, who had worked with me at Pineapple for two years, was very keen to go and live in New York. He knew his way around New York because, as a dancer, he had spent his summers there and had got to know the dance community, so I felt he was the ideal person for the job.

Of course, there are tremendous complications involved in setting up a business in another country – the legal system is different and all the relevant rules and regulations are different too. Within a few months of starting the project I had gathered a whole set of lawyers – a real estate lawyer to handle the purchase of the property, a corporate lawyer to set up the company, an immigration lawyer to sort out visas and work permits, and of course a litigation lawyer because Americans are very litigious, and you haven't really arrived until you've had your first taste of litigation!

Raising the finance created all sorts of problems, too. Pineapple had no track record in America and as far as big business there is concerned, dance is something the major corporations donate money to, not a profitable business. So I spent nine very frustrating months seeing all kinds of banks and venture capitalists and getting nowhere. Then I read an article about Michael Ashcroft, Chairman of ADT (formerly the Hawley Group), which said that he had just started investing in America.

I am a great believer in the idea that if you don't ask, you don't get, and that the worst thing that can happen to you is that the person says no. So I wrote to him and explained what we were doing, and asked if he would be interested in investing. We had a meeting at which he rather shook me by saying, 'Do you realize we already have a 4.9% stake [the maximum undeclarable shareholding] in Pineapple plc?' He suggested that we raised the money we needed for New York with a rights issue, which he agreed to underwrite via one of his companies. He also introduced us to Grievson Grant at this time who became our new brokers. Since then Michael has always been an extremely useful and supportive contact and friend.

The opening of Pineapple Broadway, almost a year later, was very exciting – champagne (Veuve Clicquot of course!), strawberries, smoked salmon and Fortnum's tea were all specially imported for the opening party. All of the New York dance community turned up, including Elena Tchernishova (ballet mistress of

ABT), Natalia Markarova and Alexander Gudonov. Twiggy and Tommy Tune also popped in as they were in 'On Your Toes' at the time.

Pineapple Broadway also received some wonderful press coverage as the media loved the fact that we were English. I was interviewed on 'Good Morning America' and 'Lifestyles of the Rich and Famous' did a programme on Pineapple.

The next step – No. 4

I had only just got back from buying the building in New York when I was driving through South Kensington and saw a 'For Sale Freehold' sign on a building which – it turned out – had started life as banqueting halls and had subsequently been a ballet school and a church! I couldn't resist going to have a look, and though it was the building that had everything – wet rot, dry rot, rising damp, a badly leaking roof – it was stunning, with marble floors, fabulous staircases and beautifully proportioned top rooms that would make a wonderful dance centre.

I thought the building in South Kensington could be a more up-market Pineapple. It was also in a good catchment area, it would mean we covered Central London with the three studios pretty well, and it would help to alleviate the fact that we were always short of rehearsal space. Added to which, I couldn't resist the building, so we decided to buy it. Like New York, it was a freehold building and this time we raised the money through the Business Expansion Scheme. Basically, this is a scheme designed to help small, relatively new businesses, by allowing investors to offset their investment in such companies against their highest rate of tax. Someone who was paying tax at 60%, for example, could invest £10,000 under the BES at a real cost of only £4,000. It's an increasingly popular scheme, and many enterprise agencies up and down the country now have registers containing lists of potential investors and companies looking for investment. Your accountant should be able to advise you on this scheme.

The clothing division

Fashion is a notoriously difficult business, so it's best to go into it gradually, as we did. In those early days, we sold a few leotards and leg warmers which were quite limited then – just white, black, pale pink and pale blue. So we found some outworkers and got them to make leg warmers specially for us in interesting colours and patterns. We were also making ra-ra skirts, sweaters and ski pants that could be worn in the studio and in the street.

And then we started telling the dancewear manufacturers how to make the leotards more exciting and stylish – cutting the legs higher, lowering the necklines and introducing new colours, But of course they were selling these exciting new lines to all their customers as well so I thought, 'This is a mug's game – we'd better start doing our own label.' So we did. It also became very clear that leotard fabrics, which were very comfortable to wear and easy to care for, could be used for street fashion, so we started developing that too.

SPOTTING THE TRENDS

I have no formal fashion training, but years of modelling gives you a feel for clothes. Also, when we were young models together in Manchester, my girlfriend Jo Apted and I could never find clothes we liked so I used to design my own and get Jo to make them up for me.

In the early eighties, street fashion was tremendously influenced by dancewear, due in part to shows such as 'Chorus Line' and 'Cats' and TV programmes like 'Fame'. Everyone was wearing tracksuits and leg warmers, and ra-ra skirts became a major fashion item.

Obviously the key to success in the fashion business is having your finger on the pulse and trying to spot the trends before they happen. But of course a fashion can die overnight, so you have to be very careful not to keep on ordering and ordering because something is selling like hot cakes. You have to be able to recognize that a fashion is coming to an end and sell off the end of your lines fast.

At sixteen, my daughter Lara is invaluable. Her age group, the mid-teens, is so fashion conscious and whereas they used to represent about 10% of the market, it's now something like 65%. All she and her friends want to do is go shopping in the King's Road or Kensington Market. They are very image conscious and are quick to sum people up wholly in terms of what they're wearing.

As for manufacturers, I found those through trial and error. People I already knew in the dancewear business would recommend factories and I'd take it from there.

We had some disasters – overstocking on certain things and then having to offload them, fabrics needed to make up orders arriving not only late but also faulty, so by the time we'd sent it back and got it replaced, it was too late to make the orders. It's all been invaluable in learning the fashion business but it does take you uncomfortably close to the edge sometimes.

GETTING THE PRICE RIGHT

Pricing is key on two points. The first one is that you need to know your market and the sort of price your customer will expect to pay for goods.

There are important psychological barriers when it comes to pricing. £15 is one, £20 is another. Under £20, you still go up in pounds – there is a difference between £16.99 and £17.99. Over £20, you might as well go straight to £24.99 because there really isn't a lot of difference. I look at a garment and think, 'This should sell at £29.99' and work backwards from there to see how much it will cost us to produce, distribute and make a profit on. If we can't make it work at that price, we don't go ahead with that garment.

Secondly your mark-up has to include your margin – your profit. If you are manufacturing your product the rule of thumb for setting the retail price is three times the cost. Suppose you buy a garment for £10, you aim to sell it at £30 – three times the cost. You then take away your selling costs which are, say, £5 and you are left with £15 profit – a margin on the selling price of 50%. If this does not cover your overheads then you must look very closely at your overhead structure.

If you aim for a 50% margin in your shop, and allow 5% for shrinkage (shoplifting, damaged stock and display and so on) and mark-down garments you have to sell at a reduced price to get rid of them, you should end up with a margin of 45%. If, when your monthly management accounts come in, your margin is only about 30%, there's something seriously wrong either with your pricing or with your stock control.

The margin you need varies according to how quickly the stock turns over; for example: a supermarket with a fast stock turn will need a lower margin and a product like jewellery where the stock turn is very slow would need a higher margin.

Pricing is key in terms of the particular market segment you're aiming at; it's pointless producing young, fun fashion if it's way out of the teens' and early twenties' price range.

The one exception is when I know we are going to sell such large quantities we can afford to cut our margins a bit. We will do a special offer in a magazine, for instance, at a lower price, thereby cutting our margins because of volume sales. The same is true with mail order catalogues. We know that we can sell, say, 3,000 of a particular dress in our shops so we need a 50% margin. They on the other hand will sell 30,000, so we can afford to cut the margin to 25% or 30%.

The infrastructure you need – the design team, the warehousing, the computer – is very expensive and in the early days you will spend more than you earn so you have to build that factor into your costings too. But fashion is a huge market and if you do get it right it can be a very lucrative business.

Export

Once you have really established yourself in this country, you will start casting your gaze further afield. We are now selling Pineapple clothing in Japan, Hong Kong, Canada, America and Europe.

Exporting can be quite a performance, but an agent will show you how to tackle all the paperwork involved, paying duty, shipping and so on. There are firms called merchanting houses who buy your goods outright and then export them on their own account, looking after the paperwork themselves. The Department of Employment's Small Firms Service, (Freephone 'Enterprise') publishes a very useful free booklet called *How to Start Exporting* which sets out all the options and, among other things, lists a number of organizations only too happy to give advice and practical support to would-be exporters.

Before you even think of exporting, you have to ask yourself what will happen if it becomes a huge success. If orders come flooding in from all over the world, will you be able to cope?

From the moment we opened Pineapple New York in 1984, the clothing got tremendous media coverage and the huge department stores like Macy's and Bloomingdale's wanted to order from us. But we've held them back because we knew we just didn't have the necessary production capacity and the distribution. If you take an order and can't deliver, people like that don't come back a second time.

Growing pains

Demand had grown so much that by the end of 1986 neither our systems nor our warehouse facilities at Covent Garden could cope with it any more. It became very clear that we had to do two things – first, find new premises and second, computerize the stock control system.

The building we took in Holloway Road, which had been a wedding dress factory and showroom, was ideal. It was closer to the centre of town than I'd hoped, and large enough to accommodate all of us – design, production, accounts, warehouse distribution, cash-and-carry and the showroom – for some years. Of course there were problems associated with the move. Some of the staff didn't want to come at all – Holloway Road has little to offer after the charms of Covent Garden or even Marylebone High Street. Some did leave while others moaned about it, but made the move. When we got there, some couldn't take the temporary chaos that is the inevitable result of a move, and couldn't see that in a few months' time it would be better than it had ever been. But the people who stayed loved it – the fact that everything was under the same roof, and we had the facilities and the space to do the job properly was more important than having to travel another few stops on the tube.

We were lucky in that our operation is relatively straightforward and the building we took over had been set up for a similar sort of business. If yours is a more complicated operation, it may well be worth your while to seek professional advice. Ann Levick and her fellow directors at PanMed, the company that makes specialist medical garments, decided when they expanded to ask the Manpower Services Commission for advice on production layout:

'It was a good decision. Having a detached, expert eye looking at your set-up and asking why you did things a particular way made you realize that there was no reason why. It was money well spent, particularly as we only had to pay one-third of the cost, and the MSC paid the other two-thirds.'

Computerization

The problems of the move pale into insignificance compared to the problems of getting computerized. As I said, the main reason for installing a computer was that our old systems of stock control, invoicing and so on, could no longer cope with the volume of business we were now doing. We also wanted to set up a system that could cope with much larger volumes of business in the years to come.

A GOOD CONSULTANT

Having made the decision to computerize, the choice of hardware (the machinery) and software (the programmes) is absolutely vital. There are all sorts of computer consultants around (good and bad). Obviously you must make sure they are completely independent, and not tied to a particular hard- or software company. But even the independent ones vary in quality. A bad one will ask you what you want, to which my reply is 'You're the expert. Tell me what I can have.' If you don't know what a computer can do for your business, how can you possibly know what you want? A good consultant will find out what your needs are, explain what computers can do, and come up with a package that best suits your needs. Your accountant will be able to advise you on both consultants and systems. The system we chose was a modified version of one we had seen in action in another company, and we had a lot of problems with it in the beginning. At one point it sent out a whole batch of invoices with every single garment at £9.99, for example!

If you're like me, and haven't much experience with computers, it's easy to let yourself be fobbed off by the experts when they say 'Oh, there are always problems when you computerize.' I allowed this to happen at the beginning – even though I'm always telling people never to assume that experts know what they're talking about, I still fall into that trap myself occasionally! If I'd made a fuss earlier, we'd have got action earlier. You are paying them an awful lot of money to do this for you, so how dare they say they usually get it all wrong to start with!

Once your system is installed, the consultant can then spend several expensive months sorting out the teething problems.

The other thing you must realize about consultants is that they are only interested in your computer. They don't mind if your orders are going out late or if the goods you're sending don't match the delivery note. It doesn't bother them that your customers are hopping mad or that you're losing not only business but good-will that has taken years to build up. 'You're putting in a computer. Don't they understand?' is their view! You can often see a dip in turnover and profits the year in which a company computerizes!

Unfortunately for us, both the hardware and the software were faulty as I had always suspected. The experts had insisted it wasn't possible but, subsequently, the computer company took the computer back and refunded the money. The battle with the software people is still going on. In spite of that fairly disastrous experience, I still believe that the right computer system is essential for a growing business, and during 1988, we computerized again – less painfully this time.

THE COST OF EXPANSION

Certainly, being computerized enables you to keep a close watch on where the money is going, but one of the problems that any business faces as it expands is that the staff become less conscious of costs. It's as though they're no longer working for a person who has to pay the telephone and electricity bills, or buy the stamps and the stationery, but for some faceless bureaucracy with a bottomless wallet! Okay, you might think it's mean to quibble about the odd personal 'phone call or stamp, but if you've got forty or fifty employees all making a couple of calls a day or posting a couple of letters at your expense, it very quickly mounts up. (You can get your 'phones 'O' blocked which means people can only make local calls, but even so they can cost enough!) Maybe huge corporations build in a contingency for that, but in a small company you can't afford to.

Pineapple by post

As with so many of Pineapple's developments, we started to do mail order simply in response to demand – people were writing to us from all over the country saying they couldn't buy our clothing locally. We also realized very quickly that magazines, quite rightly, are reluctant to feature clothes that can only be bought in London, but if you offer a mail order service they are happy to feature them.

Before you embark on mail order though, you need to do a very careful business plan. You need to know what it will cost you to prepare a leaflet (printing costs, at the very least, and if you want something a bit more sophisticated, fees for graphic designers, photographers and models too); the postage costs, staff to handle it, and as it grows, the cost of putting your mailing list and label printing on computer. It is expensive to set up and you must be prepared not to make a profit right away, but once it's up and running, mail order is a very good way of doing business.

We started in a small way with a simple leaflet and, since that proved a great success, in 1988 we produced a very stylish twenty-page colour catalogue. Many of our clothes, being stretchy, look much better when modelled than they do on hangers and seeing them being worn is a good sales aid.

With the first leaflets, we restricted the mailing list to people who contacted us. The catalogue was much more expensive to produce, but since, comparatively, it was cheaper to run off more copies, it made sense to buy mailing lists from other companies with a similar market in mind and reach more potential clients that way. It has been a huge success and I really enjoy mail order because I like knowing that we are offering the same service to people whether they live in Ongar or the Outer Hebrides as 'Pineapple people' are the same all over the world!

Licensing

For a company like Pineapple, with a very high profile and a household name, licensing – allowing companies to put your name on their product in return for a royalty – is an obvious way to expand. It's a very attractive option in several ways. It allows you to expand into areas where you have market credibility, but not the necessary expertise, and it enables you to expand at a rate which would otherwise require huge financial resources and take much longer.

It also seems like an easy way to make money – in this country the royalty is usually between 10% and 12.5%; in America 2.5% to 7% – but, as economist Milton Friedman says, there is no such thing as a free lunch.

What you are selling in effect is your name and your image, something that you have worked very hard and long to develop. They are the most precious things you have, so you must be extremely careful about the products you choose to license. You mustn't put your name on anything that isn't the quality or the market position you want or anything you wouldn't be proud to manufacture and market yourself. You must also remember that no licensee, no matter how good, will love your product as you do, and you have to be

prepared to stay very closely involved, on a daily basis
if need be, at the beginning.

LICENSING THE FOOTWEAR

In our first licensing deal with a sports shoe company,
we had control over point-of-sale material and over
advertising and promotion, but we didn't have total
control over design. They felt they knew the market
better than we did, and to an extent I believed they
were right. There was a particular style of boot I wanted
to do, but they said it wouldn't sell. I insisted that they
included it in their sample range, which they did, and
it turned out to be a best seller!

We learnt a lot from it and without it being too
damaging. By 1984 we were already being approached
to do more licensing and I think we were ready to
pursue such deals, but then Lara became ill so I stepped
back from the business for the best part of that year,
and it couldn't be pursued without me. As part of any
licensing deal, I would be expected to make personal
appearances and generally maintain a very high profile
which, of course, I wouldn't have been able to do. So it
wasn't till 1986 that someone who knew both parties
introduced us to the hosiery company Charnos. They
were facing fierce competition from their rivals and so
they wanted the Pineapple name to update their image.

LICENSING THE DANCEWEAR

In any successful licensing deal, like any happy marriage, both sides have to benefit and feel that they are
getting a good deal. If they don't, then it simply doesn't
work. Pineapple brought to the marriage its name,

design ability and great publicity, while Charnos brought the ability to manufacture quality garments, a sales force and also the ability to deliver on time. Since you can only do one licensing deal on one product line in one country, it's important that you choose your licensees carefully. Charnos fulfilled all our requirements, and what's more, since they didn't manufacture their own range of leotards, there was no clash of interests.

We produce a smaller, tighter range with Charnos than the one we have in our own shops. We're able to market test designs in our shops, and then put best selling lines into their range with just a change of colour perhaps.

Packaging is an absolutely crucial part of your image, and nobody knows more about your image than you do yourself. Your licensees might think that they know best because they're in that particular market, but they don't know best about your image.

We also had lengthy discussions with Charnos about the packaging. Initially, they wanted orange and brown pineapples and dancing girls. We wanted a simple, stunning white pack with 'Pineapple' written in pink (our corporate colour at that time), and a see-through cut-out of a body so you could see the colour of the product inside.

It's a good idea to put into the licensing agreement that they use the same graphic design company for the packaging and point-of-sale material – showcards, leaflets, posters and so on – as you do. You need to use a lawyer specializing in licensing contracts, because there is no such thing as a standard deal. Each one is tailor-made and you have to make sure that every possible aspect, even aspects that you wouldn't think of, is covered. But in the same way that accountants can't tell you what figures to put into your business plans, lawyers can't tell you what you want from the deal. You have to know what you want. Look at the size of the market, for example, and set a minimum turnover for your licensee, below which the deal becomes null and void.

Before you get involved in a deal, you must check out your potential licensee very carefully. In 1987, for example, I was looking at the possibility of licensing swimwear, though it didn't come to anything because none of the companies who approached us could produce swimwear at the right price for our segment of the market. But in the meantime, I talked to a few swimwear buyers in the top department stores and asked about the reputation of these companies. What were their deliveries like? Were they usually late? What was the quality like? You can design a wonderful swimsuit but if it falls apart the first time it gets wet, it's not only going to affect sales, it's also going to damage your valuable reputation.

TIMING

In that instance, companies approached us, but there are professional licensing brokers with a wealth of experience in arranging marriages as it were. They usually take a percentage of your royalties as their fee. As in life, one of the key elements in licensing deals is timing. A few years ago, we were approached by a manufacturer who wanted to produce our clothing for mail order catalogues. We would do the design, the clothes would be sold under our label and he would give us 5%. I said it wasn't enough, so that was that.

Instead, we pursued it ourselves, making around a 30% profit margin, which is good business. Now, having built it up, we're in a position to license that business to someone else in return for a much more sensible royalty.

The same will be true of the range of products we plan to introduce – toiletries with homeopathic ingredients. We won't license them right away. We will get them made up in small batches, sell them in our own shops and then we may do a licensing deal. People might say, 'Why give it to someone else and get only 10% when you are already making 100% margins yourself?' The answer is that someone else will be much better at manufacturing and distributing on a large scale than we are. Time is the most valuable commodity you have, so concentrate on what you do best – in our case, design and marketing – rather than spreading yourself too thinly. Is it really sensible for you to spend a day trying to resolve distribution problems in Scotland, say, when you could be using that time on something new that will take the company forward?

As far as future licensing deals go, the world is our oyster. We have a household name, a high profile chairman and an amazingly talented design team. Swimwear, lingerie, hosiery and sportswear are all obvious areas. Household goods are a bit further removed, but then Pineapple customers all have homes, so they need these things too. Customer loyalty is very important to the life of any business, and our customers are very loyal.

Franchising

In many ways, franchising is very similar to licensing. It allows a business to expand much more rapidly than it could do otherwise – as the Body Shop has shown – but it also has many of the same pitfalls. People see it as an easy way of making money – the franchisee raises the money for the business, and pays you a premium for the franchise, an annual royalty, and/or a fee for management services, and guarantees to buy all the stock from you – but it requires phenomenal management skills.

Again, what you are selling is your good name, and in order to ensure that it is not irreparably damaged, you have to have a very tight system of controls. Some of the bigger franchising companies like Body Shop and Wimpy (the hamburger chain, not the house builders) produce a management manual as thick as a telephone directory, giving detailed directions for every conceivable aspect of the business. The British Franchise Association offers helpful advice on every aspect of setting up such a business.

We have dipped a toe into the water, with one pilot franchised shop in Manchester. But we made the most major and obvious mistake. The reason franchising is so successful is that the shops are owner-run. People have their own money invested and so they want to make it work. We gave a franchise to someone with another business who wanted to put a manageress in to run it.

Sophie Mirman found that franchising wasn't the answer to Sock Shop's expansion plans, either:

'We tried it but it was too difficult to control standards. We found it very difficult to go into a shop and criticize it if it was wrong or indeed put it right. If it's one of our own shops, I'll go in myself and help them get it right, or Richard will help them give it a thorough clean if that's what's needed. Also, if it says in a franchise agreement 'You will refit the shop every three years', it can be looking absolutely ghastly, but it still won't be refitted until the three years are up. We also found it impossible to control the standard of the staff they took on. We only had two franchised shops, so we simply parted company with our franchisees on very amicable terms. It was profitable and it's a very attractive way of expanding quickly, but we simply didn't want to compromise our standards.'

For Anita Roddick's Body Shop International, though, franchising has been an outstanding success. From the granting of the first franchise in 1978, there are now around 360 franchises worldwide from Canada to Kuwait and the waiting list in this country is closed with 3,000 applicants on it. One reason it has been so successful is that the concept is very strong, stylistically and visually, making it very easy for a franchisee to 'wear it well'. Other reasons are Anita's energy and constant search for new ideas, and her insistence that each shop sets up and funds a community project.

Added to her very close relationship with all her franchises this all goes to make Body Shop an exciting, fun company to be involved with.

The idea of franchising was Gordon Roddick's, in the days before it was really established in this country. Having opened two shops successfully, they couldn't get the financial backing from the bank for a third. But they had noticed people coming into the existing shops and saying, unprompted, that they'd like to run a shop like that. They thought, 'Well you could', worked out franchising arrangements and two more Body Shops opened very quickly. It's meant that they have been able to expand at a much quicker rate than would otherwise have been possible. And since it was clear almost from the start that Anita had spotted a very real gap in the highly lucrative cosmetics and toiletries market, it was very important to become widely established before any serious competition could gain a foothold. It also gave them credibility with the banks so that they could raise the finance to open more shops of their own and to start manufacturing their own products.

The way you look . . . this year

One of our great strengths at Pineapple is image and design and we have become increasingly aware of its importance in every aspect of the business. Young people today are incredibly aware visually – they're brought up on pop videos which bombard their eyes with images. Fashions in everything from graphics to interiors change so quickly that you really have to keep a careful eye on it all and see straightaway when something begins to look old-fashioned.

Take for example, your company's logo. The trick is to change it, so that it always looks bang up to the minute and yet keep it the same because after all you must hang on to your corporate identity. With Pineapple we did it initially by keeping the logo the same but changing the colours, and then a couple of years ago, changing the calligraphy. In the early days, we had the lady with the pineapple, cream notepaper and the logo in orange and brown. After a year or so, it began to look too cosy, so the lady with the pineapple went, and the colours changed to grey and pink which were cleaner and more modern. A few years later, we went through a grey on grey phase – rather more high-tech – and in the last couple of years everything's become black and white. When I had the apartment in New York, everything was black and white – black lacquered furniture, huge white bed – and I loved it. So it reflects where I am at the moment personally, but it also reflects what's happening in the market place. There's a much less cosy, more hi-tech feel everywhere now.

The decor of the studios, and in the last year, the shops, has followed a similar evolution. In the beginning the studios were all green and white – very fresh and pineappley – and then they also became pink and grey, and now they're black and white.

We wanted a minimalist, hi-tech feel in the shops, which we have designed ourselves. They've been stripped back to basics, and we've used scaffolding poles painted black on which to hang the clothes. It's also much cheaper than expensive shop fittings, and easier to change when the time comes.

For our retail shops, we found some wonderful white mannequins which displayed the cotton lycra clothes perfectly. These mannequins constantly undergo 'face-lifts' and at present have all been sprayed gold.

Our King's Road shop presented a bit of a problem because it was very small, and though it also had a basement, it was notoriously difficult to get people to walk downstairs. They'd come in, glance at what was on the rails on the ground floor and if they didn't see what they wanted, walked out again. So we made the decision to have the ground floor purely for display purposes, and all the clothes in the basement so that customers had to go downstairs. It was a bit of a gamble, 'wasting' that ground floor space. The week after the shop opened, I drove down the King's Road one evening. All you could see through the window, apart from white mannequins, dressed in black, was a plain round glass bowl with half-a-dozen white lilies. Though I say it myself, it looked stunning and I knew the decision was right.

Anita Roddick believes that window dressing is absolutely key in retailing:

'The display in the window has to be powerful. It must shock you, and stop you in the street. It should be controversial, it should be theatre! The Japanese will hide a window for two weeks while designing it. Then when it's finished they open it to the public.'

For the first ten years, throughout all the changes of colour, the actual Pineapple logo stayed the same. The first change, in 1986, was to put it inside an oval with 'Survival of the Fittest' written round it. Then towards the end of 1987, we came up with a more graphic, handwritten 'Pineapple'. It certainly looked much more hi-tech, much less comfortable and cosy than the original one, and though I liked it a lot, it was such a departure that I had to think about it very hard. But then the way 1987 went, with so many dramatic changes for Pineapple, it really did begin to feel like the end of one chapter and the start of another, so a change of logo seemed more and more like a good idea. We started gradually introducing the new logo throughout 1988 and, as so often happens when something is right, it now seems as though it's been with us for ever!

A very good example of how design can change yet stay the same is the Body Shop. Their logo, which they call 'the pod', has remained the same, but the type faces they use have changed subtly becoming more modern while retaining the same feel. There's been a similar evolution in the look of the shops, too. What made Body Shops visually distinctive from the beginning, apart from the rainbow display of the products, was the green paintwork (chosen originally because it was the only colour that would hide the damp patches in the first shop in Brighton!), the rustic wooden shelving and the potted plants. Most people wouldn't notice how much the shops have changed in recent years because the essential elements remain unchanged. Green is still the distinctive colour and potted plants are still used, but the shelving is now also stained green, and there are green and white marbled floors and clean, white, energy-saving lighting. The design is more modern, cleaner and less cluttered.

Time is of the Essence

The more successful you become and the more your business expands, the more demands there are on your time. As time becomes more precious, learning to organize it properly and to get your priorities right becomes absolutely essential. Some people have a natural talent for this, others find that at the end of a day all they've done is respond to other people's demands and the most important thing that should have been done that day is still undone. There are now personal organizers – not simply filofaxes – but plans that actually show you how to set out your day, allotting particular time for 'phone calls, and for working uninterrupted. In theory, it's a good idea, but if someone needs a rapid response from you, and can't move until they've got it, it seems a rather inefficient use of time to keep them hanging about for an hour.

Christina Smith has tried to structure her time in this way and has found it doesn't work:

'Things happen that force you to change your plan, and psychologically that's not good. Though I do still try to set aside time for paperwork and 'phone calls, my only rule is: Do it early in the day because you never know what's going to crop up later on so you may not get it done!'

I agree. I always try to make my 'phone calls before midday. After that, I never seem to have time until after 5.30 p.m. by which time many people have gone home. I always try to see to what's on my desk as soon as I come in every morning, pass on anything relevant to the department concerned, file it for action if it's relevant to me, and bin everything else. You have to be ruthless, otherwise you soon find yourself snowed under with paper.

THE FILOFAX

Personally I find my Filofax is my bible. I bought mine ten years ago from Chisholms in Covent Garden long before they gained the 'yuppie' label. Now they're very popular and you can get them anywhere. Don't be put off by the stigma Filofaxes now have – they are still the best invention ever.

I always buy a diary with a week in view and keep

my address index at the back, along with credit cards and business cards. Don't forget the golden rule and Xerox your addresses and so on regularly. This makes the pain a lot less, should you have the misfortune to lose it. In ten years I have lost mine once – along with my passport, in a London cab – never to be seen again!

LIST IT

Like practically every other woman in business, I am a great believer in lists. At any quiet moment in the day, I'll check the list and see if there's anything I can do in the time I have, and at the end of the day, anything still not done is transferred to the next day's list. I do try to tick off every item by the end of the week, but I don't always succeed.

A great tip for dealing with lists is not to go home until you've dealt with and ticked off more items on the list than you've added that day. That way you're winning, and you get a sense of getting somewhere rather than that depressing sense of being swamped. So now before I leave the office, I check the list. If the list is the same length as it was that morning, or longer, then I don't leave until I've made the necessary number of phone calls to make it shorter.

Ann Levick of PanMed is also a great believer in lists: 'I list absolutely everything. I know it doesn't make the brain cells work, but I'd rather do that than pretend my memory is still infallible and then realize I've forgotten to do something crucial. If there's something on my desk that isn't a real priority, then I don't put it on the current list, but put it in my diary for a week or so later, so it doesn't simply get put to one side and forgotten.'

I don't use a diary as such. Instead I use black, plain ruled notebooks in which I write down everything that's happening – design ideas, notes on 'phone conversations, informal minutes of meetings. Some days I'll use six pages and others only half a page.

When the book is full, I write the dates it covers on the spine and then file it away. That means I have a complete record of every day's happenings and I can always check back if there's any dispute or confusion.

YOUR BEST FRIEND, THE TELEPHONE

I am always astonished to hear people say on 'Desert Island Discs' that what they would be most pleased to have got away from is the telephone. I am completely the opposite. In fact I think it would be my one luxury item if they would allow it, although I don't think of the 'phone as a luxury – it is a necessity!

I communicate much better on the 'phone. If you write someone a letter and something in it is not quite right, then they have to write back to you and on it goes, backwards and forwards. On the 'phone, you can jump half-a-dozen letters. However, it's a good idea to send a letter or fax confirming what was agreed on the 'phone.

The new conference calls you can make now, linking up several people in different places, are also a marvellous innovation. Before, I'd spend an hour or so getting across London to a meeting, and an hour or so getting back. Now I save those two hours. I think people are inclined to be more concise on the 'phone than they are in the flesh – they don't feel quite the same need to go through all the pleasantries – which also saves time. As for the incoming calls, ideally you will have a secretary or even a switchboard operator who can act as a filter, putting through important callers and taking messages from the rest. If you are caught on the 'phone by someone you're not ready to speak to, tell them you're in the middle of something and you'll ring them back. Don't be pressured into making a decision if you don't feel you're in full possession of the facts just because the other person is on the other end of the line. Marshall your thoughts, get together any information or papers you may need and then call the person back.

FAX IT

Fax machines are a wonderful invention and a 'must' for anyone in business. It never ceases to amaze me how your letter or sketch is fed into a machine and comes out moments later anywhere in the world.

On the Move

Mobile telephones have always attracted rather bad press. They are the butt of jokes as the status symbol of yuppies and record pluggers, and are accused by 'phone-haters of bringing stress into parts of life that other telephones can't reach! I get stressed if I *can't* use the 'phone.

I have a mobile 'phone that I can take on train journeys and I have a 'phone in the car, but only two or three people have the number so it will only ring in an emergency. I like to know that they can get hold of me if I'm the only person with a particular vital piece of information.

Having access to a 'phone wherever I am reduces 'dead time'. If you're having to wait around or get stuck in traffic you can calmly get on with your day!

WHAT KIND OF CAR?

Many people who start their own business seem to buy an expensive car immediately, even though they're not making any money at that point – as though it's part of the image!

My advice, however, would be to get a small car for running around town and resist the temptation to splash out unnecessarily on something expensive and ultra-plush! A smaller car will be cheaper to run, easier to park and less of a worry if you get the odd knock or dent.

I have always had my own car and have gone without many things in order to have the freedom you gain through having one. My first car was a white mini which, at the age of 17, I bought for £200 (I had saved all my modelling money like mad and borrowed £50 from an aunt to be able to buy it!)

For the first few years of Pineapple I had a small jeep which was perfect and was used by everyone for collecting stock, furniture and even building materials. At weekends it was also often on loan to any members of staff who were moving flat!

CABS

More often than not – and particularly in London – it is much less of a headache to take a cab if you have meetings across town during the day. It can also be a great time and energy saver as you won't have the added anxieties of not being able to find the street your meeting is in, not to mention worrying about having nowhere to park, or double yellow lines and wheel clamps! Remember, time is money and it is well worth the few extra pounds to ensure a smooth arrival and being able to free your mind of all that trivia to concentrate on more important things.

Another advantage of a cab is that, image wise, it doesn't give away your income bracket!

HIRE A DRIVER

There may also be occasions when it is a worthwhile 'time and motion' exercise to hire a car with a driver.

If you have several short appointments all around town – where it would be wasting time to wait for separate taxis or worry about parking – this can be a life saver, particularly as most hire cars come complete with a car 'phone so you can catch up on calls in between meetings. It's certainly well worth the money for special occasions or to impress important business contacts – particularly Americans or Japanese who are very image conscious.

COME FLY WITH ME

Once your business becomes international, flying will become a normal part of your travel arrangements.

One of the problems of air travel is that your fellow passengers invariably want to chat to you. A friend of mine finds the best way of coping with this is to have a personal stereo with her and put the headphones on (even if it's switched off!). Even those people who insist on chatting when you are clearly trying to read are put off by that! As for being chatted up, I've really never found it a problem and nor have the vast majority of businesswomen I know.

You read articles which say if you dress very conservatively and so on, you won't attract their attention, but I've found if I'm wearing a mini-skirt, say, that most men actually avoid taking the empty seat next to mine, presumably because they think 'She's bound to think I want to chat her up.' Most men travelling on business would rather spend the time catching up on paperwork or sleeping anyway. I also think it has a lot to do with vibes – if you are giving off signals that say 'Leave me alone', most men will.

Anita Roddick's response is typical.

'I should be so lucky! I'm forty-three years old and overweight! If people want to talk to me it's about the business. I don't come on sexy – anyway I'm far too lively and upfront to be sexy. I think you have to be fairly passive for men to want to chat you up.'

TRAVELLING LIGHT

It's so important to get organized before you pack and not to be tempted to take everything but the kitchen sink. I prefer a large zip-up, light-weight bag to a suitcase, and I travel with easy-care, cotton lycra clothes that don't crease and take up very little space. This way you can pack lots of variations on a theme, which are easy to mix and match and turn from day to evening wear – 'desk to dinner' dressing as the American fashion editors are fond of saying. Take only the essentials, remembering you are a businesswoman and not a film star; you don't need twenty pairs of shoes and six hats!

Take travel-size toiletries and make sure they are sealed well and in a good toiletries bag.

The ideal is to be clever enough to pack everything into hand luggage – especially on New York trips, where you have to queue for immigration and then wait for luggage, then queue again for customs, by which time there are long queues for cabs. With just hand luggage you sail through and make a streamlined exit into a cab. It also looks more business-like if you have one smart bag, rather than lots of clutter. Porters are often difficult to find too and, if you are not being met, heavy luggage is, literally, a drag.

JET-LAG

When I started travelling between New York and London regularly I discovered a new challenge to contend with – jet-lag!

How could I avoid losing valuable time while my body time-clock and sleep patterns adjusted to the time difference?

Dr Sharma's wisdom once again provided me with the answer – he told me to wear brown paper bags on my feet during both flights!

It has something to do with circulation and being earthed, and stops your feet swelling, but never questioning his advice I tried it and it works! I've never had a problem since. You scrunch ordinary brown paper bags (the sort tomatoes come in) around your bare feet and put your socks and shoes back on over the top. Don't worry – you soon get used to the feeling of wearing them and the utter disbelief of your fellow passengers!

I went to New York with Arlene Phillips a few years

ago, and when I put my bags on she said 'You really are embarrassing to travel with', and tried to pretend she wasn't with me. We were invited to two opening nights that week, with dinner afterwards on both occasions. Both nights, Arlene fell asleep half-way through the performance, never mind the dinner, while I was wide awake. She then had to fly to LA to do an all-night video session with Olivia Newton-John, so I persuaded her to try it. She did, and is now a devotee. She never flies anywhere without her brown paper bags!

When you're flying it's also a good idea to drink plenty of still mineral water and avoid alcohol which is very dehydrating. Having said that though, on the night flight home I usually knock back a couple of glasses of champagne or white wine to help me sleep. It's also important when you're flying long distances to put your watch straight on to their time. I'm sure it doesn't help if you're always thinking. 'Well, it's really lunchtime for me, not breakfast time.'

Anita Roddick agrees and always drinks lots of water, avoids alcohol, and is a great believer in aromatherapy oils:

'I rub them on my chest before I get on the plane and stick my nose down the front of my blouse at regular intervals for a reviving sniff. I also have lots of aromatherapy baths when I get there. I then work through until it's bedtime wherever I am, and so far I've never suffered from jet-lag.'

Sophie Mirman has no tips on avoiding jet-lag. She just doesn't suffer from it:

'In fact Richard and I were only saying as much one Monday morning when we had flown back from New

York the night before. Then Richard touched his face and realized that he'd forgotten to shave!'

TRAVELLING ALONE

I have been interviewed by journalists on the problems of businesswomen travelling alone and I've had to say I really couldn't help because as far as I'm concerned it's not a problem. You stand much more chance of being upgraded on a plane if you're alone for example. I also once enjoyed a British Airways flight back from Paris to London in the cockpit because the plane was over-booked, and that certainly wouldn't have happened if I hadn't been travelling alone. As far as I'm concerned, there are more pluses than minuses in travelling alone in business.

HOTELS

I've never found staying in hotels alone a problem either. Reception staff are often more helpful when you are alone, and as for dining alone, I personally choose not to eat in the hotel restaurant, not because I'm afraid of being chatted up or given a rotten table, but because, to me, the height of self-indulgence is to order a meal from room service and eat it lying in bed watching television.

Going Public

Do you really want to go public?

By the end of our third year, 1981, Pineapple was doing very well. We had two dance centres, Covent Garden and West, the clothing side of the business was a great success and we had doubled our profits each year. It was very clear that the demand and the opportunities to expand were enormous.

I was very keen to open a studio in New York, and I also wanted to build up the clothing business and start wholesaling, which meant I needed bigger premises and a distribution system to get the goods out. The problem was raising the money. I already had personal guarantees on the leases of the two studios and it was getting to the point where it wouldn't have been wise to borrow any more from the banks. Then an old friend and a very successful businessman, John Sadiq, suggested that we went public – in other words raised the money we needed for expansion by selling shares in Pineapple to the public.

There are other equally good reasons for going public. In Anita Roddick's case, there were three:

'First, we were now having to fight for good sites and we were up against giants like the Conrans of this world who are eating up High Streets everywhere, so we needed the high profile that going public brings. Second we wanted our staff to have a stake in the company, and third, the garden, which is my pride and joy, needed paying for!'

Initially, Sophie Mirman and Richard Ross weren't at all sure that they wanted to go public:

'We had been approached by a number of stockbrokers keen to handle it, and our own financial advisers told us that at some stage we ought to look at the possibility of a flotation. But we weren't sure. It was our company, did we really want to sell part of it off to other people? It took us about a year to get round to it, and I'm very glad we did. It's enabled us to expand in ways we couldn't even have contemplated before.'

The USM

We chose to go public via the Unlisted Securities Market which was set up in 1980 and is run by the Stock Exchange especially for smaller businesses seeking to raise money for expansion. The main differences between the USM and a full listing on the Stock Exchange are that with the former, you don't have to sell more than 10% of your equity to the public, which is obviously an advantage if your company is young and growing very rapidly, whereas with the latter, you have to sell a minimum of 25%. You also need five years' trading record for a full listing, and the cost of 'going public' via the USM is considerably less.

In order to qualify for the USM your company must be a public limited company, and must have a trading record of at least three years.

A SPONSOR

You must have a sponsor to co-ordinate the complicated business of complying with all the rules and regulations and also to manage the marketing of your shares. In our case it was John Robertshaw of Energy Finance (now York Trust) and our brokers were Coni Gilbert and Sankey. Since Big Bang, and the blurring of divisions between stockbrokers and the merchant bankers, it can be either, though if your sponsor isn't a member of the Stock Exchange, you'll need to employ a stockbroker to liaise between your company and the Stock Exchange.

To attract a sponsor, you will need to show that you are operating in a field where there is plenty of room for a growing company like yours, and that your company is soundly based, with good prospects of future growth – for example, that your profits have doubled each year. In our case, we had gone from £20,000 to £40,000 to £100,000 in three years. These days, you are unlikely to attract a sponsor unless your last year's profits are over £250,000.

THE COSTS

Since your sponsor will be recommending your share to his clients and the public, he has to be sure that your company is all it seems, so you will need reporting accountants (your own accountants usually acting jointly with one of the large firms such as Coopers & Lybrand) to prepare a detailed report of the company's financial situation, on the basis of which your sponsor will finally decide whether or not to go ahead. You will also need solicitors to handle all the legal aspects of going public. Obviously, along with the other heavyweight professionals you need – accountants, your sponsor and a stockbroker if your sponsor isn't a member of the Stock Exchange – it is a very expensive operation. In 1982, it cost us £70,000. Two years later it cost the Body Shop over £100,000 and in 1987, it cost the Sock Shop a staggering £400,000.

If your company is making millions, it's a relatively small sum, but in our case it was the best part of one year's profits. It's also a risky business in the sense that you don't know until the last minute whether or not your flotation will be allowed to go ahead. There have been cases where something has been found to be not quite right with the company's records, or the market changes, and the flotation has been aborted. That means not merely a lot of money down the drain, but it is obviously a pretty shattering blow to the image of the company concerned. For this reason some small businesses will either opt for a merger or allow themselves to be bought in by an existing public company. As long as you're prepared to make the transition from proprietor to manager, it's a quicker, cheaper, safer route.

Going public is a very time-consuming business. It took over six months of meetings to sort out all the details, including the track records of the directors and key personnel to, finally, setting the share price.

Setting the Share Price

The share price is worked out according to a number of factors. First of all, there's the condition of the Stock Market as a whole. Then there's the view the market takes of the industry your company is in, along with the past record and future prospects of your company compared to other similar companies. The standing of your sponsor can make a difference, as can other competing flotations.

The issue price is usually set slightly below the level at which the sponsor expects the shares to start trading. It's reckoned that on a small flotation, a premium of 5% to 20% on the issue price when trading starts indicates that the pricing was about right. There have been many examples in the last few years where the shares have started trading much higher than that, but it doesn't mean necessarily that the brokers got it wrong and underpriced the shares. They have a responsibility to maintain an 'orderly market', and so have to fix a price that can be reasonably maintained in the longer term after the initial excitement had subsided. It would do little for their own or the USM's reputation if they priced the shares too high, so that they started trading lower than the issue price, or soon fell below it once the initial flurry of interest died away.

DON'T GET SHORT-CHANGED

However, you should make sure that the broker doesn't deliberately underprice the shares to make him look good and to short-change you! You have to remember that, although technically the broker is working for you, his success depends on big institutions buying the shares he brings to the market. If he offers them an attractive deal, then they will look more favourably at the next deal he brings them. And what's an attractive deal to them may not be such an attractive deal for you.

In our case, the shares were pitched at 52p each. It was decided to issue one million shares, and since we needed to raise around £200,000, to offer 400,000 of them (40% of the company) for sale.

A small quantity of shares was available at the issue price to staff, teachers and friends. As with all shares, there was a risk that when they went on sale to the public, there'd be few takers and the price would go down, so they would lose money. But all the indications were that on the first day of trading, they would close higher than the issue price, which would be a very nice little bonus for the people who'd taken us up on the offer.

Some people keep some of the money they raise as a well-deserved reward for years of hard work, but I ploughed every penny back into the company. Norris Masters (who I was then married to) was an accountant and became involved at this stage on the financial side of going public. He insisted that he should have 50% of the remaining 600,000 shares, so they were divided equally.

In the case of the Body Shop, the aim was to sell 20% of the company's equity and raise £1 million. So the stockbrokers concerned fixed the share price provisionally at 85p. Quite late in the day they realized that, unlike most other share flotations where the demand for shares is only considered in terms of the general public and the big institutions, the Body Shop had an additional group of potentially very interested share-buyers – its franchisees. A meeting with them, along with the company's employees, made it very clear that indeed they did want to invest heavily, and as only 10% of the shares to be sold had been allocated to employees, there obviously wouldn't be enough to go round. So it was decided to raise the share price to 95p.

In April 1987, 20% of the Sock Shop's equity was floated on the USM. The share price was set at £1.25, opened on the first day of trading at £2.60 and raised around £2 million for the company.

Remember, Remember

The day Pineapple was floated on the Stock Exchange, 5 November 1982, is a day I'll never forget. We were asked to take some dancers along and the brokers had covered the stand with pineapples and ballet shoes. It was a real media event. I was the first and only woman Chairman ever to be allowed onto the trading floor at the Stock Exchange, and only the second woman to visit it (Her Majesty, Queen Elizabeth the Queen Mother having preceded me by just a few weeks). Every single paper and TV station turned up – or so it seemed – all fighting to get into the tiny Stock Exchange press box. We were in all the TV news bulletins, on the front page of the *Evening Standard* and in all the national dailies the following morning.

The share issue was over-subscribed several times, and at the end of the first day's trading, the share price was £1.00, almost double the issue price of 52p.

For Sophie Mirman, too, the publicity that resulted from the Sock Shop going public was invaluable:

'I'm sure that the increased business that resulted from all the publicity easily covered the £400,000 it cost us to go public. Although most of the publicity was on the City pages, don't forget we have a lot of shops in the City!'

When Pineapple started to run into difficulties in 1984, I was accused in certain newspapers and in the City of having 'hyped' our share price up. But that just isn't true. The whole world of the City was new to me and I wouldn't have known where to start 'hyping' a share price. Of course, we were glad of the publicity – every broker wants good publicity for a launch because it reflects well on them – but there is no way you can plan for the kind of coverage we had. It just happened. It was as though the market itself wanted such an event. We opened the door for companies that might previously have been considered 'frivolous' – fashion, marketing, entertainment and so on.

THE THIRD MARKET

Perhaps if the Third Market had been in existence when we went on to the USM in 1982 it might have been a more attractive option for us. Designed for small companies which are either too new or too small in terms of profits to meet the guidelines laid down for the USM, or indeed companies which are rejected by it, it is less complicated and therefore cheaper both to enter and to operate in. You still need to be sponsored by a Stock Exchange Member Firm. If you don't know of one personally, your accountant or banker will almost certainly be able to recommend one.

The Pluses

With all the media coverage we had had since we first opened in Covent Garden, we already had a high profile, but certainly going public made Pineapple a household name and increased its status in the world of business. As Anita Roddick says, a company is never successful until the City says so, and that's what going public means. It also creates a lot of confidence in your company. People doing business with you know that before the Stock Exchange accepted you into the USM, your company would have been rigorously investigated and found to be financially sound.

A couple of years after they went public via the USM, the Body Shop applied for and got a full Stock Exchange listing, partly to gain even more credibility, and partly to create a wider market for their shares, since some institutional investors are limited in the number of USM shares they can hold.

OUR FIRST RIGHTS ISSUE

As I've already mentioned, our main reason for going public was to raise money to expand the business. Later on, our public status made it relatively easy to raise the finance for further expansion. When we decided, in 1983, that we wanted to open in New York and couldn't raise the finance there, we raised it through a rights issue here. This means that you issue extra shares and offer them to existing shareholders, usually at slightly below current market value.

How many shares you offer depends on how much money you want to raise. If your company has one million shares with a market value of £2 each, and you want to raise £1 million, you, need to issue an additional 500,000 shares. These are then offered to shareholders in direct proportion to the shares they already hold. If someone holds 10,000 shares – 1% of the existing one million shares – you offer him the chance to increase his share holding to 15,000 shares, that is, 1% of the new total of 1.5 million shares.

We increased the number of shares in Pineapple from one million to 3.6 million, and so, as I held 300,000 shares originally, I was entitled to increase my holding to over a million shares. But to buy some 700,000 shares would have cost a vast amount of money which I didn't have, so I just increased my stake a little. That meant that I was no longer the majority shareholder in Pineapple, but then nor are chief executives and chairmen of many multi-million pound enterprises. While in theory you are more vulnerable to a takeover, that is very unlikely to happen as long as you are successful and doing well by your shareholders.

If there are any shares not taken up by existing shareholders in a rights issue – the rump, as it's called, is taken up by your underwriters who either hold on to them or sell them on to a long-term investor.

The Minuses

With hindsight, I think Pineapple was probably too small and too young to go public because suddenly the spotlight and the pressure were both on us to deliver the profits. For example, if we had still been a private company, and we had raised the $2 million needed to buy a freehold property in New York, and had spent several hundred thousand dollars converting it into the biggest dance studio complex in the world we would have fully expected to make a loss for a few years. But as a public company you can't do that. The City (not to mention your shareholders) expects you to come across with the profits and if you don't, your share price suffers! Being a public company certainly clips your wings.

If Richard Branson's Virgin group had gone public before he launched his airline, Virgin Atlantic would never have happened. The shareholders and the City institutions would have taken the view that a man who ran record shops knew absolutely nothing about running an airline, and so such a venture was sheer foolishness. Indeed when Virgin did go public, the City wasn't interested in the airline, so Virgin Atlantic wasn't part of the package. It stayed private, and ironically makes a bigger profit than the other side of the business. (Incidentally, since Richard Branson has re-privatized the Virgin Group, many people who had sympathized when I went private early in 1988, thinking that something terrible had happened, suddenly realized exactly what I had done and began to congratulate me instead!)

But perhaps the major disadvantage of going public, and something that I certainly didn't take into account beforehand, is that you suddenly become closely involved in the City. You have to learn a whole new range of skills very quickly. You are going to institutional lunches, you are going to meetings with your brokers, you are preparing annual reports and gearing up for the AGM, you are giving presentations about your company to institutions – the pension funds and so on who are going to invest in your company. That's not just a one-off thing either because not only do you have to make sure that the existing ones keep on investing, you also have to have new institutions informed. And all the time you're doing that, you are not doing your most important job – running your company. What you really need to do is employ someone at a senior level to deal with the City and leave you to get on with what you're best at. I certainly didn't think it would be clever to try to do both.

Anita Roddick finds that side of the business less than fascinating, too, but Sophie Mirman actually enjoys it:

'Richard and I share it, and I actually rather like it because it means we're talking about something we love. If our institutional investors want to come and see the operation, that's fine. I rather like showing it off!'

Hitting Problems

Despite all the drawbacks of being Pineapple plc, our first year as a public company was pretty successful, and in July 1983 we made a pre-tax profit of £155,657 – not bad considering the costs involved. At the beginning of 1984, we had bought the building on Broadway for Pineapple New York, and through the Business Expansion Scheme, we had bought Pineapple Kensington and the builders were moving in to start work in both places. Things were going extremely well and it was a very exciting time. One of the greatest rewards for working hard is the encouragement and recognition you receive, and it was at this time I had the honour of being invited to Number 10 to a 'Reception for Success' held by Mrs Thatcher.

However everything was about to change.

It was only hours after this memorable evening in February 1984 that Lara's school had telephoned to say she had become seriously ill. Although I tried to keep up appearances, the fact was I simply couldn't give the company the time and commitment it needed and Pineapple's problems began. The company's growth was steadily upwards until the beginning of 1984, and after that, it started to go downhill. Without me running the business it couldn't grow, it could only stand still. Pineapple was, after all, my dream, I was the innovator, the designer, and it was entirely up to me to determine the future. In business, if you stand still, you end up going backwards. Our costs – rent, rates and so on – went up, but profits didn't, so it wasn't long before we were making a loss.

Certainly some of the problems were due to external factors, and would have cropped up anyway, but I honestly believe that if I had been on the spot, I would have been able to tackle them right away, before they became too serious.

THE BANDWAGON

All the publicity we got when Pineapple went public was marvellous but in some ways it made it sound as though this ex-model had just opened a dance studio and made a million overnight. As a result, along with the popularity at this time of 'Fame' on TV, musicals like 'Chorus Line' and 'Cats', and the 'Fitness Boom' – the world and his wife decided to jump on the bandwagon and open dance studios.

Also, in the beginning, we'd been virtually unique in the sort of casual clothing we sold. Suddenly, you could buy leotards and track suits everywhere.

In order to stay ahead of the competition in business you have to move very quickly on to the next thing. That creative input had always come from me, and for the best part of a year I wasn't really there to provide it.

MANAGEMENT STRUCTURE

It also became very clear during that year that Pineapple had no proper middle management structure – something that is essential for any company that is to grow. Over the years, Pineapple had evolved from being a small, almost family business where everyone mucked in, into a successful growing company that needed a good management structure. During that year, what lines of reporting there were all but disappeared. There was a lot of overspending on stock, and bad buying! We would run out of absolute basics like black cotton tights, and be left with boxfuls in colours nobody wanted.

To run a successful company, it's essential to set up a structure that can operate without you. Anita Roddick, for example, has her 'Red Dot system':

'Anyone within the organization whom I know I can trust to keep the firm's integrity intact has one, and they're left to make decisions when I'm away.'

CONFIDENCE

For any business, confidence is the key, but that is especially true of a public company. If the market begins to lose confidence in a company for whatever reason, its share price starts to slide, shareholders panic and start to sell, so the price slips even further. It's a frightening downward spiral. Christina Smith agrees:

'You have to put a brave face on your business. In the bad times, you can't hide away. I don't mean you resort to trickery, but you do have to get up in the mornings and get on with it. I can remember, in the seventies, my boss Terence Conran saying in a radio interview that Habitat was having a hard time, and the next day all the creditors rang up and demanded payment, which of course made the situation much worse. In business, confidence is critical.'

You owe it to your shareholders to keep confidence high, and that's one reason why I tried to prevent news of Lara's illness becoming public knowledge by returning important 'phone calls from home and attending public functions where I would have been notable by my absence.

Getting back to normal?

Lara went back to school, although still not fully recovered, in September 1984 but then my husband Norris became seriously ill that autumn and had to go into hospital. With the additional worries and pressures that this inevitably caused it was well over a year before I was back in the business full-time, not merely physically, but mentally and emotionally too.

Although as I've said, in some ways Lara's recovery left me feeling exhilarated, that it was a miracle that she had pulled through and that no problem would ever seem as daunting again, the whole episode had drained me to such an extent that when I did start trying to pick up the reins of the business again, I found that my confidence had gone. People who'd been running Pine-apple while I was away, had got used to doing their own thing, and when I'd ask about something, they'd say 'Don't worry about that, I'm dealing with it.' To be honest, I was just so thankful that people were still there that I just wasn't as tough with them as I should have been.

I felt I needed help to sort the business out fast and instead of doing what I usually do and asking around, I used a specialist retail fashion recruitment agency to find me a team. It was an indication I suppose of how exhausted I was that I didn't follow my own golden rule and assumed that 'experts' knew what they were talking about. I allowed myself to be swayed by the 'I know this business, I know what I'm talking about' approach. They might have known better about 'this business' but they certainly didn't know better about mine!

The result was not the solution of existing problems but the creation of new ones. One person I took on, for instance, got us involved in contract manufacturing – getting unbranded clothing made by manufacturers we didn't normally use for the large mail order catalogues which we also supplied with 'Pineapple' clothing. If it had all worked as promised, it would have made us a lot of money. If it didn't – if goods were not up to standard or were delivered late and were rejected by the catalogues – then we would be left with vast quantities of clothing that we couldn't sell through our own shops. And that is exactly what happened. Not only did we lose money by being horrendously over-stocked, but what was almost more serious was that it affected our relationship with the catalogues.

Norris had fortunately recovered from his illness towards the end of 1984 and decided to participate full time in Pineapple at the beginning of 1985. Our marriage meanwhile had undergone many serious pressures and problems which led to our separation in February.

Although some of the papers blamed my involvement in the business for the break-up, I believe that without Pineapple to engage me and keep me busy, the marriage would have ended sooner than it did. This complicated business matters still further.

Soon after we separated, Norris sold some of his Pineapple shares to buy a dance shoe manufacturing company. The last thing Pineapple needed at that time, having reported a loss the previous year, was for large amounts of shares to be unloaded onto the open market, since the City would assume there must be more bad news on the way and the share price would fall still further. But that is precisely what happened. As if that wasn't bad enough, we were 'gazetted' at around the same time, with the result that our bank lost confidence and withdrew our working facility.

Cash flow problems mean profit problems. We couldn't afford to pay our suppliers on time, so deliveries were late and we lost business as a result.

THE LONG HAUL BACK

Pulling yourself up out of a hole is much more difficult than starting from scratch. You have to work like crazy to get back to Square One, and you're spending time and energy on putting out fires that you ought to be spending on building up your business.

I never panicked, even when the going got really tough, because it's not in my nature. Besides, what's the point? If you are panicking, your staff are hardly likely to remain calm and confident, and if everyone is running round in circles, the net result is that your business does the same and inevitably collapses.

Cut costs and tighten up

When you hit problems, the ability to organize your time and sort out priorities is a life-saver. You have to be able to stand back, look at the problem areas and decide which need tackling first. You can't deal with them all at once – some will have to be shelved.

Obviously what you must concentrate on first are the money-making areas. Cash flow is the life-blood of your business.

If you find that sales are dropping, don't assume you know the answer. Go and investigate.

Scrutinize every corner of the business. If something is starting to sell more slowly, cut the price and get rid of it. We have a permanent sale basket at Covent Garden. Any discontinued colours and end of lines go in there. Even if you have to sell the odd thing at cost, or even at a loss, it's better to keep the cash flowing than to have it tied up in unsellable stock.

Look at your staff costs and assess what people actually do. It's true that work expands to occupy the number of people available to do it. Often one person can do what two people are doing and achieve more because they are more focused.

TIME AND MOTION

Be very mean with your time. It's flattering to be asked to various lunches and receptions, but you have to think not only of the time there, but also the travelling time and, if you're expected to make a speech, the preparation time too. You can really only afford that amount of time when your business is running smoothly and the cash is flowing.

Becoming acquisitive

I began to feel that I was getting back on top of the business which had unquestionably slipped away from me during my absence, but I knew that as far as the shareholders and the City were concerned it was going to take too long for Pineapple to start delivering the kind of profits they expected. They like to see quantum leaps, not just a few per cent rise each year.

As we were subject to all the pressures and expense of being a public company the obvious move was to use this status to broaden our base by acquiring companies.

Peter Bain had been a non-executive director of Pineapple since early 1984, as a result of Michael Ashcroft underwriting our first rights issue. In late 1985 an opportunity arose for him to join us as a full-time director. The timing was perfect as his experience with Michael Ashcroft and the ADT group in the acquisition was to prove to be invaluable in the development of Pineapple Group.

Having decided to embark on an acquisition strategy, the first thing to do was to define the new area of potential activity. A number of new market areas were investigated with one in particular becoming increasingly attractive the more we investigated it – Marketing Services. As an industry it is relatively new, and only started to find its feet in the mid-70s. It covers sales promotion, design, direct marketing, exhibitions, premium gifts, incentives, and so on, which all come under the umbrella of marketing services. There seemed to us to be an opportunity to put together a Group that offered all these services.

Once we had decided that this was the direction the Pineapple Group should take, the next thing to do was to restructure our balance sheet so that we could move forward. We went to our shareholders in mid-1986 and asked for further funds via another rights issue. We were looking for companies that were of an appropriate size, had good management, that were prepared to stay and work with us, were cash generative and had the opportunity of showing further growth over the years ahead. We were not looking for companies that were in trouble, that needed turn-around management (as we did not have these resources), or even 'green field' start-up situations. In November of that year we made our first acquisition. It was a company called Golden Key Promotions Ltd. It had taken us many, many months with nearly eighty investigations of possible acquisitions completed before we found a company that fitted the criteria we had set ourselves. During this time the costs were borne by the existing Pineapple business.

Finding The Money

You might think that with Pineapple making a loss and the share price down, it would be impossible to raise the money to expand, but Pineapple is a household name and as far as the City was concerned, Peter's track record on acquisitions was first class. The combination of the two made it possible.

As I have said, we approached our shareholders for further finance, via another rights issue, which meant we were then in a position to do deals with cash and shares. We structured our deals on the future profitability of companies, only paying a relatively small amount of the total purchase price on Day One, with the balance being paid as the companies made the profits. In a sense, the companies you acquire make the money to pay for themselves.

ACQUISITION FACILITY

If you find a company which you wish to acquire amongst all those you are offered, you have to move quickly, as obviously you won't be the only interested party. For that you may need to arrange an acquisition facility with your bank, in other words permission to go into overdraft, if you need cash to acquire the company quickly. Once the deal is done you can always go back and sort out more appropriate long-term finance for the deal.

We had run into problems with our existing bank, so we moved to one of the new American banks which had opened up here, but soon after we did so they changed their small business policy and the acquisition facility they had promised us disappeared. We moved bank again, and got the acquisition we needed, but the move cost us over £50,000. We sued the American bank and recovered our costs.

As soon as the word gets round that you are looking for acquisitions, details of all sorts of companies come your way. In the early stages unfortunately these opportunities are almost exclusively those that nobody else wants, and mostly in industries or disciplines that you don't wish to invest in. In our case there was an assumption, because of the name and history of the company, that we would look at fashion companies, health clubs, health food restaurants and so on. Manufacturing and catering were certainly two areas we were not interested in.

Once Golden Key joined the Group, its direction became more clearly defined which made further acquisitions a little easier. In February 1987 Premium Pen joined us – they are one of the largest premium gift suppliers in this country. April saw Keymark Out & About Ltd come into the Group. Keymark specializes, like Golden Key, in free hotel accommodation-based incentive packages. In May of that year we acquired Regent Leathergoods, complementing Premium Pen in that they manufacture a whole range of leather products directed at the premium gift market. To round our financial year off, we acquired two New York Manhattan-based companies, BMS Marketing Services, a sales promotion agency, and Infinite Image, an audio/visual conference and seminar organizer.

At the end of that year, we were able to report a profit of £1.254m against the loss of the previous year and a Group that was now once again on safe ground.

We were making great progress and we knew it

wouldn't be long before the objective of creating a one-stop marketing group became a reality. People observed that we were obviously going for the commodity end of marketing services, but that was just not true. We were equally interested in moving into design, sales promotion and direct marketing when the opportunities arose.

In October 1987, the so-called market 'melt-down' happened. We had to re-assess our strategy. In spite of this, in early 1988, we acquired 'Graphiking', a very aggressive design company, and 'The Wallace Group', a US-based company, which is probably one of the world's largest sales promotion companies.

The profits for the year ending July 1988 were £4.1 million, and Prospective Group, as it's now called, is well on the way to becoming one of the largest international below-the-line marketing groups.

Going Private

When Pineapple went public, as in many cases, a new holding company was formed called Pineapple Dance Studios plc which in turn bought the shares of my original company, Pineapple Dance Studios. In 1985 when we started looking for acquisitions this company was still the only operating subsidiary the group had. It had taken eighteen months to find the first suitable company to acquire in November 1986 but the next six here and in the USA had followed pretty quickly and by the end of 1987 Pineapple Dance Studios was one of seven subsidiaries.

PRESSURES

During this time it was becoming clear though that the original Pineapple business was being swamped by marketing services and was not sitting very comfortably in the group. The heads of the new marketing subsidiaries were beginning to find that clients were confused about the name Pineapple and would say 'what have marketing services to do with Debbie Moore and fitness?'

We had already decided to sell the building in New York. Its value had almost tripled in three years and the return on the investment could no longer justify having around £3.5 million tied up in a property. It made commercial sense to sell it and use the proceeds to invest in more acquisitions.

The board had even begun to talk about the possible disposal of the fashion business and the studios in London – the core of the business that I loved! They didn't share my commitment to the dance community – the reason I'd started Pineapple in the first place – and there was no reason why they should. They were not a philanthropic organization. They were running a business and their major responsibility was to maximize profits for the shareholders.

In the six years since Pineapple had gone public, I found myself under a great deal of pressure – not only pressure from the City to deliver profits, but personal pressure, too. My private life was not only public property, it could also have an effect on the share price. That was why it was so important to keep Lara's illness a secret which only added to the stress we were already under. In the City, being the mother of a child who was seriously ill would have been seen as a weakness – something, I suspect, that wouldn't happen to a man in the same situation.

As I have said, Pineapple had also begun to suffer while we were building up the Group. It really does need a lot of love and attention and I felt the time had come to remember my advice at the beginning of this book – being in business is tough and it's much easier to be tough if you enjoy what you do and care about it.

And as Sophie Mirman said:

'You can't enjoy building up your business if your only interest is your bottom line profit.'

Buying Pineapple Back

It was beginning to be clear that the best thing to do as far as I was concerned was to buy Pineapple back. If I took the company back to private ownership it would give me back the freedom I had lost to develop the business I love in the way I wanted, away from the spotlight and pressures of the City. It would allow me to settle, in the short term at least, for a business with comparatively small profits, something which as a public company you simply cannot do.

It is much harder to be creative and entrepreneurial when you are a public company, and that's the kind of business I wanted to run – one that I could move in any direction that interested me.

It made sense from the shareholders' point of view too, because the marketing services side of the business was now making healthy profits and the side I wanted to buy back was in fact making losses, reducing those profits.

Having decided to buy back Pineapple, the first step was to find out if it was feasible. Touche Ross, the City accountants, came in to give an independent valuation of our assets, i.e. stock, leases, debtors, and a review of our liabilities so that a price could be determined that I would have to pay Pineapple Group.

As it was still making a loss, I felt the price was unlikely to be very high. They also had to put some kind of valuation on the name 'Pineapple', but as it had been so closely associated with me since the very beginning, I couldn't imagine it would be worth very much to anyone else without me.

Telling the world

We made our announcement by issuing a press release on 26 November 1987 stating that I intended to buy back the studios, the fashion business and the Pineapple name for an 'as yet undisclosed sum'.

Press reports appeared on 27 November. In the *Evening Standard* 'Pineapple's Debbie steps out of City', and the *Guardian* 'Debbie back in Private Sector'. In *Today* it ran:

'End of An Affair for Pineapple

'Former model Debbie Moore is preparing to quit the stockmarket. She is poised to buy her Pineapple keep-fit and dancewear company back from public ownership for a nominal sum.

'Although her deputy chairman and live-in lover Peter Bain will take over the quoted below-the-line marketing business, there is no question of a domestic rift, say sources close to the company.'

The deal was now well and truly in the spotlight which attracted several interested parties – one of whom happened to be Norris Masters, from whom I was now divorced.

The next day he issued a press release saying that spurred on by press reports claiming that I was going to buy the studios for a 'fairly nominal value', his company was willing to pay a proper commercial price for the Pineapple name and assets. This resulted in more press reports in December: *The Independent* 'Masters bid for a slice of Pineapple'; *Daily Mail* 'A Pineapple Split'; and *The Times* City Diary (no less!) wrote:

'Does Moore's move mean the end of her affair with Pineapple chairman, Peter Bain, and a reunion with Masters, father of her child? "No chance," says Masters, "I'm living with a very nice lady and am very happy." Moore's London house is, on the other hand, up for sale!'

All this had very little to do with the business. The story was also inaccurate, both in fact and in implication. I was still chairman of Pineapple and while it's true that the house was on the market, it was simply because we had bought the house next door for its larger garden and parking space!

For the whole of December 1987 it seemed as though my life was just one long meeting with lawyers and accountants – we had to spend a great deal of time on every aspect of the proposal.

In the early stages, the board and I had both been using Pineapple Group's accountants and lawyers to work out the deal. But then I realized that, in fact, I was starting out all over again from square one and, as I have said, when you're starting in business, you need a good lawyer and a good accountant of your own. Mike Bowler from Harbottle and Lewis, who'd been lawyers for Pineapple Ltd since the beginning, sorted out the legal details, but I needed to find a new accountant. As so often happens in life, timing is all. As soon as I'd decided to follow my own advice, I had a phone call from Robert Coe, of Wilder Coe Management Consultants, saying he had read about what I was trying to do and offering to help. Ironically they were Pineapple accountants when we started. He and the other partner from the original firm, Ian Wilder, were in fact enormously helpful during that whole time, and their new partner, Stephen Brookner, became Pineapple's finance director.

By the beginning of December 1987, Touche Ross had fixed the price at £1. It's the sort of figure that is considered a bit of a joke, but in fact the calculations were extremely complicated and all sorts of factors had to be taken into account. For example, it was eighteen months before the Pineapple Group made its first acquisition, so the expenses incurred – salaries and overheads – in building up to the acquisition of the portfolio of companies contributed to Pineapple Studio's losses during that time.

We had also supplied Pineapple New York with clothing which had never been paid for because they were trading so close to the line, but as that business was staying within the Group until it could be sold, that debt also had to be taken into account.

The price of £1 included a huge, inter-company debt of £500,000, comprising the losses made over the last two or three years which Pineapple Group had subsidized, and which I would have to take in.

I also agreed to waive my profit-linked service contract as chairman of the public company, which would have been worth a lot of money over the next four years. Had I stayed where I was, I could have made a very comfortable living without working anything like as hard as I'm working now, so no-one can accuse me of doing what I did in privatizing the core of the business for the money!

THE EXTRAORDINARY
GENERAL MEETING (EGM)

An Extraordinary General Meeting of the shareholders
was called for 21 January 1988, at Pineapple West, to
vote on the sale of the core business to me. In accord-
ance with the rules and regulations of public companies,
a circular detailing the proposed deal had been produced and sent on 5 January 1988 – at least fourteen
days ahead of the EGM – to all the shareholders, along
with proxy voting forms to allow those who couldn't
attend to cast their vote by post.

The proxy votes started coming in overwhelmingly in
favour of the deal, but even so I couldn't relax because
someone could have turned up on the day waving a big
cheque, and if it had been a serious offer, we, the board
of Pineapple Group, would have been duty bound to
consider it.

The big day arrived and the EGM was held at 10 a.m.
in Studio One at Pineapple West. Again the papers
reported on the result of the EGM and the soap opera it
had turned out to be. On 22 January 1988 the *Guardian*
reported:

'Pineapple Saga's Debbie Wins Custody of "Love
Child". *Guinnesty* may have the big names in the City
soap opera ratings, but for glamour, showbiz razzle and
personal interest you can't beat the Pineapple saga.

'Yesterday's episode saw City heart-throb, Debbie
Moore, get custody of her love child, Pineapple, though
she only had £1 to spend, while her ex-husband Norris
Masters was written back into the plot at this time, as
he offered to buy Pineapple at a commercial rate.

'He arrived for the EGM only to be told that his offer

was not high enough and to see Debbie's offer of £1 overwhelmingly accepted by shareholders.

Not a dry eye in the house!'

Followed by *The Times*:

'The Pineapple Group soap opera reached a melodramatic conclusion yesterday when a sparsely attended EGM passed the deal by which Debbie Moore agreed to sever her financial connections in exchange for a £1 purchase of the Pineapple Dance Studios. The only vote against came from Moore's former husband Norris Masters.'

The City press had a lot of fun and looking back I can see the joke, but at the time the pressure was enormous. The possibility of a more acceptable bid was always there – as there is in any 'buy out' – but perhaps more so as we had attracted so much attention. Of course, buying Pineapple back was a risk, but I honestly believe that there are few things worth having in life that aren't.

Re-assessment

As soon as the deal went through a period of six months' consolidation was needed. However it was during this period that I was spending most of my time with Lara as she battled with her second illness including some time in New York for her operation in August. Her recovery was slow but sure and after daily physiotherapy and swimming she began to regain her strength and was ready to return to school in November.

Once she was on the road to recovery, I was able to take a long hard look at the business I now owned. As the business had been losing money, the first thing I had to do was increase the revenue and cut down on the overheads. As I've said before, wholesaling was the part of the business that gave me the most hassle and the least fun. So it made a great deal of sense, now that we had established ourselves in the market, to concentrate on retailing and mail order. Without the wholesale business, we no longer needed huge warehousing space, so we sold the lease of the premises on Holloway Road, making a profit at the same time.

The business was now consolidated with the dance and fitness centres thriving and the clothing becoming more and more in demand.

The group (plc) continued trading as Pineapple as it took some time to come up with a new name, but they were finally renamed Prospective Group in June 1988, and at this time moved away to completely independent offices.

By the autumn of 1988 I had given all the centres a facelift, built a new management team – a mixture of old and new faces, and there was a great feeling of renewed energy.

Ready for Marriage

Pineapple is a household name when it comes to health, fitness and fashion. The licensing route is an obvious next step, and with our name and high profile together with our design and P.R. ability, we will be marrying up with companies who have expertise in manufacturing and distribution. This way the services Pineapple has to offer will be more accessible to our customers across the country and worldwide. There is already great interest not only in this country but also from America and Japan.

My first trip to Japan in Autumn 1988 produced some serious interest in a major licensing deal with one of the largest corporations in the world on a whole range of products.

Incidentally, no-one about to do business with the Japanese should leave home without having read *Dealing with the Japanese* by Mark Zimmerman (George Allen and Unwin). It's full of the most fascinating insights and invaluable advice. Most of us would never realize, for example, how important the exchange of business cards is to the Japanese, and that it is a ritual. When someone hands you a business card, you take it in your right hand, with a bow, then study it carefully, and bow again, acknowledging that you've read it before you put it away. By taking it and putting it straight in your pocket as you might well do here, you would offend the giver deeply and rule out any chance of doing a deal.

The Toiletries Project

An exciting project in the pipeline is our range of toiletries. Over five years ago I started to work with Dr Sharma to formulate a range of toiletries using homeopathic ingredients. The products are designed for people in a hurry – a shampoo with a built-in conditioner, bath gels – a revitalizing one and a relaxing one – and a marvellous, all-purpose cream based on arnica, calendula and urtica. The latter was originally formulated to treat cuts, burns and bruises, but has now become my universal, desert-island product and I use it for everything from sunbathing and aftersun cream to hand cream and eye make-up remover.

Market research is currently under way, with a launch planned for summer 1990.

Onwards and Upwards

Looking back at Pineapple over the last ten years in the course of writing this book has been a very valuable exercise for me. I'm not the sort of person who enjoys dwelling on the past – today and tomorrow always seem more exciting than yesterday – but reflecting on the mistakes we've made, and the problems we've encountered along the way (as well as the successes, of course) has only gone to confirm the many lessons that I have learnt the hard way – from experience.

If I were to draw up one of my lists of pluses and minuses for these ten years, the latter might well be longer than the former, what with all the problems, both professional and personal, that I have had to deal with. But quality is more important than quantity, and in that respect the pluses far outweigh the minuses. Starting, running – and indeed rescuing – my own business has given me more pleasure, more fun, more excitement, more satisfaction than anything else I can imagine, except perhaps seeing my daughter Lara well again. I have travelled the world, been to some extra-ordinary places, and met some fascinating people from whom I have learnt, and am still learning, a great deal.

I am often asked 'Knowing what you know now, would you do it all again?' and the answer is, unhesitatingly, 'Of course!' In a way I am starting again, and I find the prospect very exciting. Where will Pineapple be by the time we celebrate our 20th birthday? I don't know, but I can't wait to find out . . .